Hostas

Sandra Bond

WARD LOCK

First published in Great Britain in 1992
by Ward Lock Limited, Villiers House,
41/47 Strand, London WC2N 5JE, England

A Cassell Imprint

Text filmset in Cheltenham
by Chapterhouse, The Cloisters, Formby
Printed and bound in Spain
by Graficas Reunidas, Madrid

Distributed in the United States by
Sterling Publishing Co., Inc.,
387 Park Avenue South, New York, NY 10016

Distributed in Australia by
Capricorn Link (Australia) Pty Ltd.,
PO Box 665, Lane Cover, NSW 2066

British Library Cataloguing in Publication Data.
A catalogue record for this book is available from the British
Library.

ISBN 0 7063 7060 0

Frontispiece:
**_H. sieboldiana_ contrasting in form with
Miscanthus sinensis 'Silver Feather' and the
unusual _Campanula bononiensis_.**

Contents

Preface

Twenty years ago the number of hostas readily available was in single figures. Today there are more than a thousand and although a large number of these will only be found in specialist nurseries, an ever-increasing range is finding its way into gardens. This book is in no way an attempt to list every hosta available but to indicate the importance of this genus in the context of garden design. I have tried to cover a wide range of situations where hostas have an important part to play and to appeal to the gardener planting hostas for the first time as well the enthusiast looking for newer varieties.

Hostas, with their superb foliage, are easy to associate with other plants and in today's smaller gardens are a boon to most mixed plantings. They will thrive in the shade cast by trees and shrubs, covering the dying foliage of early bulbs. Foliage plants last much longer than flowers, but a garden that is only foliage can be too static; it is the interplay of foliage and flowers that can make a garden a special, individual place, and hostas have an advantage in that they are foliage plants which flower. Massed hostas can look superb, but they also enhance a wide range of plants and in their turn are themselves enhanced by contrasting foliage such as ferns.

Like any plant, hostas should be selected in relation to the fundamentals of climatic and soil conditions, as it is far better to use plants that suit the situation than struggle with a particular plant in adverse conditions. Often, hostas can be grown in containers where the control over their needs is greater; they make excellent architectural plants placed in containers on shady patios. I grow hundreds of specimen hostas in pots for exhibiting and many flower arrangers who need pristine leaves have also found that this is a very satisfactory method, so I have tried to cover cultivation and problems in pots as well as in the garden.

I have touched on the problems of nomenclature but only so that the gardener is aware that problems exist and that name-changing will go on happening as we study the genus in ever greater detail and realize plants have been misidentified in the past.

To some extent this book is an attempt to put in writing the answers to the many questions I am asked, and to give ideas for plant associations using a wide range of hostas. It is a guide to the possibilities, as the most effective design has elements of surprise – the personality of the creator superimposed upon the limitations of the site. I hope that your appreciation of hostas will be further enhanced and that this will help you to decide which ones to plant and where to place them in your garden.

S.B.

H. **'Silver Lance' echoing the white variegation on** *Acer negundo* **'Flamingo' underplanted with** *Aruncus aethusifolius* **and ferns.**

CHAPTER 1

Foliage in Design

Foliage plants have an important place in garden design; they set the scene and can act as the framework to plants with less determinate form. Foliage comes in all shapes and sizes, evergreen and deciduous, and it is the interplay between the similarities and contrasts that result in effective design.

A totally evergreen garden can appear very static, rather dull and lacking in surprise, whereas a garden with no evergreens is deprived of winter 'bones' so the aim should be for balance and harmony. The shape, size and colour of foliage all influence design; contrasting and complementary leaf shapes have a part to play – a large round leaf underplanted with a small round leaf, a plain leaf against a frilly one. Very large plain leaves rest the eye and act like full stops; they can complement the scheme (although large pinnate leaves need much more care in use and should not be over-used).

A bamboo towering above a group of hostas introduces not only a contrast in size and shape but in density of leaf. It appears airy and graceful and sets off the solidity of the hosta to perfection. Vertical plants are a vital element in designing a garden. Too many and the effect can be heavy; not enough and the planting looks flat and uninteresting. Low level accents can be achieved by irises, day lilies, grasses, Solomon's seal, and higher ones by the larger bamboos, grasses such as *Miscanthus sinensis* 'Variegatus' and some ferns.

In the ideal plan all plants should harmonize, in reality it is better to make small groups into pleasing compositions at different times but the restrictions of soil, climate and aspect must always be considered. In the long term plants that suit the conditions will make the most satisfactory gardens. Hostas will grow in the sun but with very few exceptions will not look their best: the leaves will develop brown edges, they will become dormant early, and as there are so many plants that revel in dry sunny conditions, why struggle? Hostas are basically shade plants, some tolerate more sun than others and some even need more but they are not sun lovers. It is far better to accept the physical limitations and to design accordingly. What are often seen as difficult situations can, with the right plant material, become a positive advantage. Foliage and form are not enough if the plants will not flourish; it is far better to grow them in containers if the required conditions cannot be met. A very wide range of plant material can be grown this way. Good design goes hand in hand with plant knowledge; the combination of artistic flair with an understanding of fundamentals can result in designs of outstanding beauty. Remember when planning and planting that schemes need time, as plants do not generally reach maturity in a season.

Hostas as important foliage plants

Hostas have a restful quality; they act like full stops and create a cool oasis and are one of the most important foliage plants. There is an enormous range in size, shape and colour and although they are also flowering plants it is the foliage that is the dominant element in design.

Hostas are generally easy, long-living perennials that associate with many other plants. As their season of interest is from spring through to autumn, the most successful use in small gardens is often in the context of mixed planting. A framework of trees and shrubs will give the light shade conditions that hostas revel in; bulbs can give colour in the very early months before the leaf canopy develops and contrast in form for the rest of the season can come from grasses, ferns and other perennials, giving an interesting all-year-round garden.

Existing shade, such as in the shadow of a building, is ideal for foliage borders; they need not be dull as foliage comes in many shapes and colours. The variation in the hosta leaf can be exploited, the plain green, grey, gold and blue leaves being just as important as the variegated ones, although there is no doubt that variegated hostas are planted far more in gardens, despite the fact that an assortment of variegated leaves is not easy to mix successfully. Used well, variegation in plants acts like a highlight, and a predominantly shady green corner of ferns, for example, can be brought to life by the addition of a green and white hosta such as H. 'Francee'.

Variation in hostas

Hostas come in a wide range of sizes from miniatures 5 cm (2 in) high to towering 1.2 m (4 ft) mounds, but the very tiny hostas do not have the impact upon design that their larger brethren have. Some mounds are spreading, others upright and this is another aspect that can be exploited. H. 'Krossa Regal', for example, is vase-shaped and can be planted as an accent among lower-growing plants, whereas a smaller variety such as H. 'Ginko Craig' looks much better planted in larger numbers as an edging.

The leaves come in four basic shapes: round, lanceolate, heart-shaped and triangular. Some are wafer-thin while others are thick in texture; some have flat margins, others wavy. The leaf can be cupped, twisted, puckered, dimpled or flat, and present many different surface appearances: matt, glossy, leathery or glaucous, and each leaf surface giving a different effect as the light catches it. If all these variables are considered with the many combinations of leaf colour (blue, cream, gold, green, grey and white) and size it is not so surprising that there is now a very large range of hostas available.

Although hostas are primarily foliage plants they do flower, their elegant flower spikes or scapes usually appearing through the latter half of the summer. The flowers range from white to deep violet, and some are delightfully fragrant. H. 'So Sweet', one of the newer varieties, has beautiful scented white flowers in late summer above a green and cream-edged mound of foliage and, like all scented hostas, has been developed from H. plantaginea. One of the present breeding aims is to increase the range of fragrant hostas as this is a very worthwhile improvement.

Gardeners can exploit the diversity of hostas to achieve many different effects, but it must be remembered that the immature plant often bears little resemblance to the mature hosta: the leaf is narrower, the colour is not fully enhanced and the variegation less pronounced. Hostas should be left alone for the first three or four years to grow and mature; constant chopping up means that the mature leaf form is never allowed to develop.

CHAPTER 2

Hostas as Garden Plants

In their native habitat hostas do not grow in deep shade but on the margins of deciduous forests, on rocky outcrops and even in the open in damp grasslands. They are partly hidden in the vegetation and in order to flower and set seed they need some sun. They are not being used as foliage plants, so the visual appearance of the leaves is not important. Gardeners growing hostas as foliage plants would like to keep the foliage in pristine condition, and the ideal for most hostas is filtered shade, adequate moisture and feeding; full sun and dried roots is a recipe for disaster – leave these sorts of situations to Mediterranean-type plants. Green and gold hostas will stand more sun as long as they are not dry at the roots, but blue hostas maintain their colour far longer with more shade. The blues have developed a bloom to the leaf to protect against spring sun before the leaf canopy develops and this disappears as the summer advances when it is no longer needed, but if these are grown in the shade of trees and shrubs then the blueness is retained for most of the summer. This is why blues look much bluer in shade.

Some hostas can be grown in dry shade as long as they are established and, ideally, mulched and naturally strong-growing. The less the shade the more essential that the moisture level is adequate. The plants will not be as luxuriant but some will grow surprisingly well where little else will. In very cool climates where the temperatures are rarely high and the sun weak many hostas can be grown in the open as long as there is adequate moisture. A few very thick-leaved hostas such as *H.* 'Sum and Substance' will stand full sun but these are the exceptions. If in doubt plant in the shade.

Micro-climates often exist in gardens. A large shrub rose, for instance, will create a partially shady, cooler spot underneath, even though the roses are in full sun, and hostas can take full advantage of this. *H.* 'Halcyon' associates wonderfully with old-fashioned pink and white shrub roses and their abundance of foliage lets the hosta grow in a relatively shady position. As long as the sun of late spring is not abnormally strong *H.* 'Halcyon' is quite happy until the leaf canopy develops. It is the versatility of the hosta that has made it one of the most popular perennial plants today.

Hostas can be used in various ways in gardens – in hosta borders, in shady corners, on the margins of ponds, as ground cover, on alpine beds and in containers. They can be used on their own or in association with a wide range of plants that enjoy the same conditions.

Hosta borders and walks

Very keen growers of hostas tend to have a hosta border or even a hosta walk. There is so much variation in hostas that they can be grown together, contrasting and complementing each other. I personally prefer a shrub and tree backdrop and a modest use of other flowering and foliage perennials that maintain the cool effect but add contrasts of form rather than colour.

Gold and greens. *H.* 'Geisha' with the cascading mounds of *Hakonechloa macra* 'Aureola', the gold tones picked up by the mats of *Lysimachia nummularia* 'Aurea'.

The shade provided needs to be light rather than dense so that some light filters through, and the competing roots from other plants not so greedy that they take all the moisture and goodness from the soil. Such conditions could exist in light deciduous woodland and the border or walk created by edging a path with hostas. A shady house or garden wall border will also give an ideal site as long as it is not bone dry. If planting hostas in a prominent position in the garden it is probably best to use them with discretion as they are primarily summer plants and hosta borders will by their very definition not be interesting in the winter. It is possible to use bulbs that like shade as underplanting, but it is important to remember that hostas like a rich diet and this does not suit snowdrops, for example.

Enthusiasts who become collectors of hostas are happy to accept the need to create near to ideal conditions, erecting artificial means of shade to achieve this without the worry of competing tree roots and problems of seasonal variation. At its most attractive this can be a specially constructed tunnel or pergola with light but closely spaced members to give filtered light; wooden laths are often used in the USA, especially in nursery demonstration areas. They can be made into handsome structures. Trade growers usually use net tunnels covered in plastic and giving 50 per cent shade, as these are far cheaper and give enough light for golds to colour and enough shade for the white-edged varieties not to burn. Artificial protection achieves other benefits such as wind protection – wind can burn leaves just as the sun can – and late frosts are not as damaging in shady areas.

By growing hostas in close proximity, cultural needs are met far more easily and frost cloth can be rolled over the plantings if unseasonal weather occurs in late spring when the emerging shoots are most prone to damage.

If a large number of hostas is grown together great care is needed in the juxtaposition of the different varieties. Making the most effective use of hostas by leaf colour is discussed more fully in the next chapter, but the most satisfactory grouping is to place the gold and green-gold variegated forms at the opposite end from the white variegated ones, and to use greens and blues in between. Highlights among the blues can come from H. 'Frances Williams', a blue with a wide yellow-beige edge, or H. tokudama 'Aureo-nebulosa' with a cloudy yellow centre to its bluish leaf. H. 'Bright Lights', an even brighter gold-centred H. tokudama form, would fit beautifully where a border is changing from gold to blue. H. 'Snow Cap' and H. 'Regal Splendor' could be planted nearer the white end; these two very new hostas which will become popular, have white edges to blue-green leaves. There are so many attractive hostas of varying shades of plain golds, blue and greens to set off the variegated ones, and green hostas are just as effective as the variegated forms and much under-used.

When variegated hostas are associated with each other great care is needed and it is important to keep to a limited spectrum and a similar leaf shape. H. fortunei 'Aureo-marginata', a medium green with a yellow margin is reflected on a much smaller scale by H. 'Golden Tiara' and if plain yellow and green varieties are placed in the same group a satisfactory picture will be achieved. There is an enormous variation in the shades of blues and greens and this can be exploited by picking up the subtle differences in adjoining plants.

Sometimes less than satisfactory groupings have to be made as the collector needs to find a home for the latest treasure. Lance-shaped hostas can be the most difficult to place but if used together the similarity of leaf shape acts as a common denominator, over-ruling any discordant elements.

Some hostas are so dramatic, they make wonderful specimens. A single plant of *H.* 'Sum and Substance', which has enormous chartreuse-gold leaves, can be placed as a 'full stop' in a predominantly gold planting of much smaller varieties such as *H.* 'Golden Prayers' which should be used in larger numbers as an underplanting. Hostas at the edge of the border look much better if planted in generous numbers of a limited range, as they give the border cohesion.

If hellebores, pulmonarias and small daffodils are planted towards the back of the border these will give interest in the spring; *Narcissus* 'Thalia' is especially effective with the emerging shoots of hostas.

Shade gardens

Hostas are ideal shade plants and can be planted in areas that often present problems. In recent years many gardeners have realized that hostas not only grow in shade but they thrive there, and the part of the garden that was the least favourite place can become the most attractive in the garden. Instead of bemoaning the problems of shade, some gardeners start to plant more trees and shrubs in order to create new shade beds for the increasing number of hostas, hellebores and ferns, to name but a few of the plants that they now wish to collect.

Moist shade is far easier to deal with than dry shade but because the sun does not dry out the soil at the same rate of evaporation as in the open, dry soil in shade is usually cooler, and with the addition of humus and mulch many hostas can be planted with a wide range of other plants.

Figure 1 is of a woodland glade with some parts drier than others, and the plants have been selected accordingly. The shade is cast by existing deciduous trees and shrubs and by the planted evergreen shrubs, which in this instance are viburnums, sarcococcas, skimmias and camellias as the soil is neutral. The hostas act as foils to the shrubs and are associated with other perennial plants which enjoy the same conditions.

DRY SHADE

It is possible to have a bed in dry shade that is as interesting as the rest of the garden; it will not be very colourful as very few brightly coloured plants thrive but it will be all the more effective because it is restful and in keeping with the ambience of shade. Many established gardens have a large tree where very little seems to thrive but in many instances the ground can be completely covered virtually up to the bole. Trees that leaf very late are not suitable for hostas as the leaf canopy will not give protection to the young hosta foliage, and those that have extensive surface roots can be too greedy; planting just beyond the overhanging branches will be more successful if the tree is a dense evergreen such as a large holly.

Good soil preparation is needed. Organic matter helps to retain moisture; this can be manure or home-made compost, and leaves should not be cleared away but allowed to rot down to make leaf mould. When planting, adequate holes must be made among the surface tree roots and as much moisture-retaining composts incorporated as possible. The plants need to be thoroughly watered in and ideally mulched to retain the moisture, but if no mulch is available pulling dry soil over the wet is better than nothing, and will prevent direct transpiration.

The first season of planting is critical. Plants must make adequate root systems so that they will be able to withstand future periods of drought – often the only moisture that penetrates is that in the months when the tree is not in leaf. Old, established clumps of hosta have stood droughts remarkably well without any

watering although the leaves have become smaller in places where the lack of rainfall has been extreme and the water table has dropped to very low levels. Many strong-growing hostas will be perfectly happy; they will not be as large but will make more than satisfactory mounds.

Figure 2 shows a suggested planting plan for a dry, shaded bed. In my garden I have a very large oak tree; the soil below its wide canopy is dry but the accumulated leaf mould of many years has helped to improve the structure. The only plants originally growing there were a large colony of double snowdrops and some woodland anemones which I have left. *Luzula sylvatica* 'Marginata', *Geranium macrorrhizum album* and *Helleborus foetidus* were planted near the tree trunk and have established a complete ground cover. *H. undulata* 'Albo-marginata' (*H.* 'Thomas Hogg'), *H. undulata* 'Univittata', *H.* 'Francee' and *H.* 'Ginko Craig' were all then planted in groups where their white-variegated foliage gives highlights. Blue and green hostas used include *H. lancifolia*, *H.* 'Candy Hearts', *H.* 'Blue Boy', *H.* 'Blue Wedgwood' and *H.* 'Halcyon' for areas near the edge of the bed and *H.* 'Blue Angel' (a *H. sieboldiana* type that does not have cupped leaves) and *H. fortunei* 'Hyacinthina' for larger mounds. Very cupped hostas such as *H. tokudama* and *H.* 'Sea Lotus Leaf' are best not planted under the drip of trees as their leaves collect debris that falls from the tree.

Plants for winter–spring interest include bergenias, which need to be carefully placed slightly away from the hostas, hellebores, pulmonarias, snowdrops, and

Frontyard bed in the garden of Warren and Ali Pollock in Wilmington, Delaware, USA. Hostas left to right are 'Antioch', 'Roseanne' (a new yellow), *fortunei* 'Aureo-marginata' with 'August Moon' behind and 'Sum and Substance' at top left.

Iris foetidissima. Additional vertical accents are from the repetitive planting of *Iris foetidissima* 'Variegata', an invaluable plant for the winter garden and a fine contrast in form and colour against blue and green hosta clumps. As the season advances Solomon's seal (*Polygonatum × hybridum*), dicentras and foxgloves are followed by aconitums and Japanese anemones, and then a carpet of cyclamens.

The degree of moisture varies enormously in areas of shade. Nothing will grow under very dense established evergreen trees such as a yew as moisture never penetrates, but in areas that are dry in the summer and get some winter rainfall, there are many plants that will associate with the hostas and are invaluable. *Arum italicum* 'Pictum' is particularly effective in the winter and spring garden with its delightful silvery veined leaves which completely disappear when the drumsticks of red berries (which are poisonous) push up in the autumn. *Euphorbia amygdaloides robbiae* with its dark green leathery evergreen leaves, luzulas and symphytums will clothe areas that are just too dry for the hostas. Some of the *Dryopteris filix-mas* forms will grow surprisingly well in dry shade and make interesting contrasts with the hostas, as will *Tellima grandiflora* with its creamy green spires of tiny flowers.

Invaluable evergreen carpeters, which can act as 'markers' to the hostas in the winter months so that a fork is not inadvertently pushed into the crowns, include *Ajuga reptans*, epimediums (although these need their old leaves cut away in the spring so that the flowers can be appreciated), small leaved ivies, lamiums, pachysandras, tiarellas and vincas (periwinkle). All will colonize dry shade as long as they are given a good start and a mulch applied when the soil is moist or it has been watered.

If the soil is dry because of walls or buildings it is much easier to plan, as the angle of the sun will

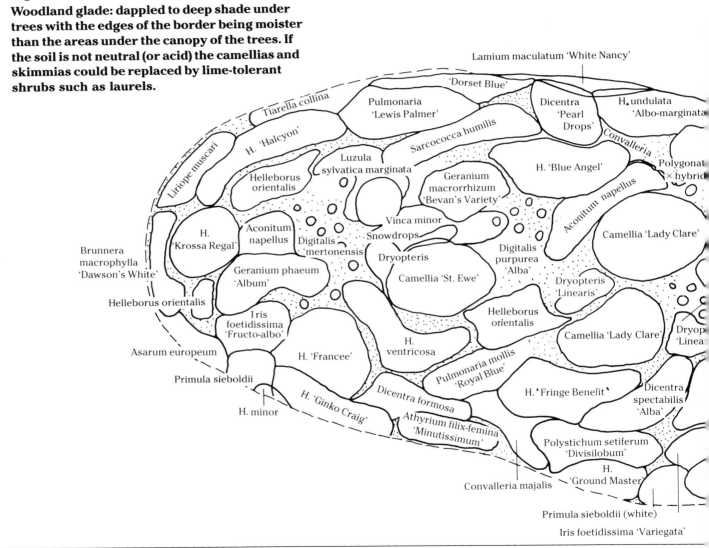

Fig. 1
Woodland glade: dappled to deep shade under trees with the edges of the border being moister than the areas under the canopy of the trees. If the soil is not neutral (or acid) the camellias and skimmias could be replaced by lime-tolerant shrubs such as laurels.

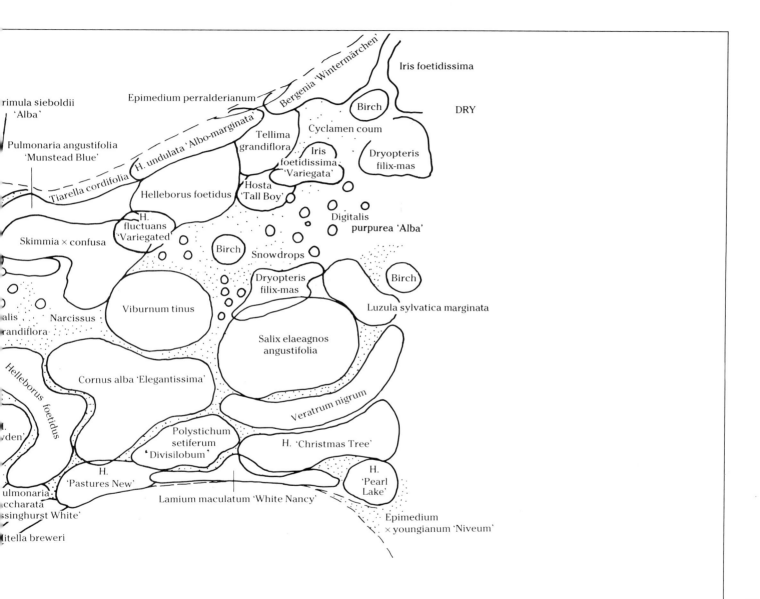

rimula sieboldii
'Alba'

Pulmonaria angustifolia
'Munstead Blue'

Epimedium perralderianum

Bergenia 'Wintermärchen'

Iris foetidissima

Birch

DRY

Cyclamen coum

Tellima
grandiflora

H. undulata 'Albo-marginata'

Iris
foetidissima
'Variegata'

Dryopteris
filix-mas

Tiarella cordifolia

Helleborus foetidus

Hosta
'Tall Boy'

Digitalis
purpurea 'Alba'

H.
fluctuans
'Variegated'

Skimmia × confusa

Birch

Snowdrops

Dryopteris
filix-mas

Birch

Luzula sylvatica marginata

alis
randiflora

Narcissus

Viburnum tinus

Salix elaeagnos
angustifolia

Helleborus foetidus

Cornus alba 'Elegantissima'

Veratrum nigrum

den'

Polystichum
setiferum
'Divisilobum'

H. 'Christmas Tree'

H.
'Pearl
Lake'

H.
'Pastures New'

ulmonaria
ccharata
ssinghurst White'

Lamium maculatum 'White Nancy'

Epimedium
× youngianum 'Niveum'

itella breweri

Fig. 2
Dry shade under the canopy of an established
tree such as an oak which gets winter rain but
where very little moisture penetrates in summer.

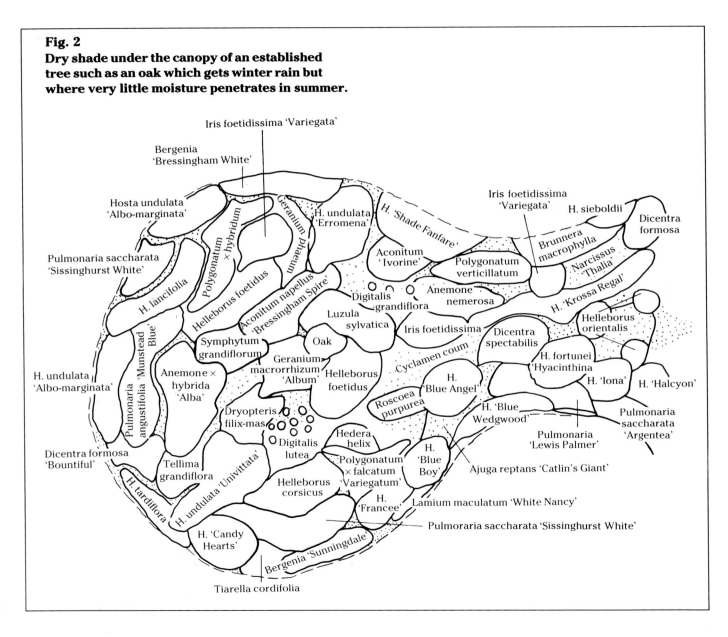

determine the degree of shade at any given time in the year and many more hostas can be successfully established as long as adequate soil preparation and watering are given. Gold and gold-variegated hostas are best planted in areas of more light but most of the others will be happy. Some, especially the blues, happily grow in areas where the sun never penetrates. The leaves will be fewer but larger, and the flowers more sparse.

MOIST SHADE

Moist dappled shade is the ideal habitat for hostas and the range of plants that can be used in association with them is very large. Many of the plants that will tolerate dry shade will luxuriate in damper conditions, although not all are suitable. Here the massed effects of drifts of plants blending with each other and with the hostas will achieve their zenith. The principle of planting in drifts applies as much on the large scale as on the small. All planting schemes need linking plants, groups which are often at the edge to tie the design together. Hostas are one of the best of the perennial plants for this purpose. Chosen carefully they can bring order to chaos, but the slightly wild effect should not be lost altogether; the ideal looks natural, but has been carefully contrived by the selection of the plant material. This is the place for blues and greens with a judicious use of variegated forms.

Figure 3 is for a cool scheme which could also be used in a damp border in the white garden, the purist removing the flowers from the hostas. *Matteuccia struthiopteris*, the ostrich feather fern, is a superb architectural plant as long as it is not placed in a windy situation and associates beautifully with many hostas,

Previous page:
H. undulata 'Univittata' at Wakehurst Place, Sussex, UK. This will establish in dry shade.

providing a contrast in form and leaf. The white edges of H. 'Francee' and H. 'Ginko Craig' are accentuated against the lacy plumes and the lower-growing fern *Polystichum setiferum* 'Divisilobum' with its much darker green fronds sets the hostas off to perfection. The finely cut foliage of *Aruncus aethusifolius*, with tiny creamy-white spires of flowers reminiscent of an astilbe, peeps out from under the mound of H. 'Francee'. *Heuchera cylindrica* 'Greenfinch' (*Heuchera* 'Green Ivory' would be equally effective) with its taller spikes of greenish bells completes the picture as it is far happier in cool, moisture retentive soil although it will grow in drier soils.

In a sheltered, moist, partially shaded corner *H. montana* 'Aureo-marginata' (this hosta is the first to emerge and can be damaged by frost) could be the focal plant for a late spring group with *Dicentra spectabilis* 'Alba' which seems to need moister soil than some of this family, *Primula* 'Dawn Ansell', a lovely double primrose that flowers for weeks in spring, *Geum rivale* 'Album', a diminutive water avens, and *Milium effusum* 'Aureum' (Bowles' golden grass). Astrantias, ferns, *Smilacina racemosa*, *Primula sieboldii* (preferably a white form) *Lilium martagon* 'Album' and *Kirengeshoma palmata* would all associate with the hostas for continued interest through the season. H. 'Ground Master' and H. 'Golden Scepter' could be used as edging hostas in generous numbers as these also emerge earlier than most.

A completely different effect is achieved by planting *H. sieboldiana* or one of the many other large blue hostas in generous drifts with *Astrantia maxima* which has glistening pink flowers, Solomon's seals, and pink and white astilbes (they flower for much longer in partial shade and do not need as much moisture as when planted in the sun). Plants for interest early in the season are plum-coloured *Helleborus orientalis*, *Ophiopogon planiscapus nigrescens* and pink

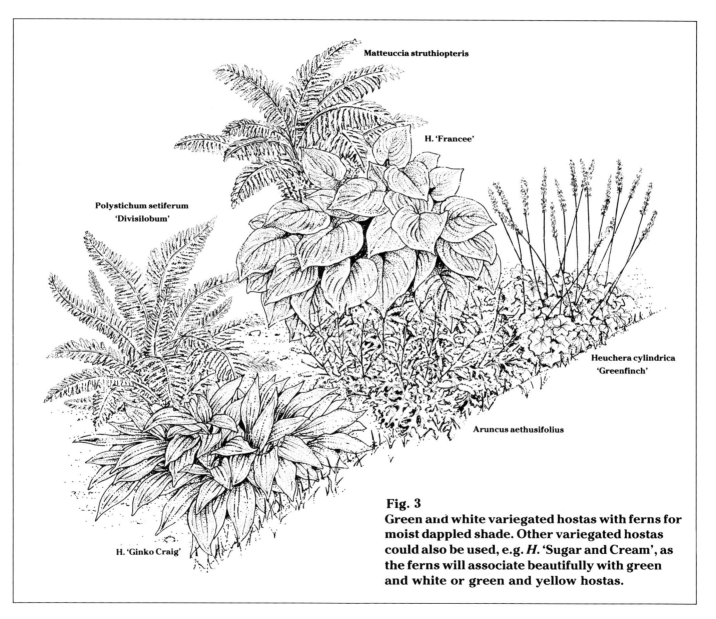

Matteuccia struthiopteris

Polystichum setiferum
'Divisilobum'

H. 'Francee'

Heuchera cylindrica
'Greenfinch'

Aruncus aethusifolius

H. 'Ginko Craig'

Fig. 3
Green and white variegated hostas with ferns for
moist dappled shade. Other variegated hostas
could also be used, e.g. *H.* 'Sugar and Cream', as
the ferns will associate beautifully with green
and white or green and yellow hostas.

erythroniums. *H.* 'Halcyon' underplanted with *Pulmonaria longifolia* or one of the newer very silvery pulmonarias such as *P. saccharata* 'Tim's Silver' and *Astrantia major* 'Rubra' could also weave in and out towards the front of the border. *Viola labradorica* with its small purple leaves and propensity for self-seeding is excellent for ground cover under the mounds of blue hostas, as are the tiarellas and *Ajuga reptans*.

Plants for vertical accents include bamboos such as *Phyllostachys nigra* and *Sinarundinaria nitida* (*Semiarundinaria nitida*) or, on a smaller scale, aruncus, cimicifugas, filipendulas and veratrums. The variegated hosta for this border could be *H.* 'Christmas Tree' planted in front of a group of *Veratrum nigrum*. The tall stems of near-black flowers would create a dramatic focal point in late summer and echo the purplish black tones of *Ajuga reptans* 'Atropurpurea', *Ophiopogon planiscapus nigrescens* and *Viola labradorica* which are used for ground cover. The hosta enthusiast could add many more smaller hostas with blue-green foliage such as *H.* 'Hadspen Blue', *H.* 'Blue Moon', *H.* 'Dorset Blue and *H.* 'Blue Boy' and a few with variegated leaves such as *H.* 'Frosted Jade' and *H.* 'Iona'.

HOUSE BORDERS

Shady patios and corners of buildings need bold, architectural planting. It is often better to use only one hosta variety and to contrast this with other plants. If very dry the choice of plants is more restricted than if the moisture is adequate, but, as can be seen from the plants shown in Figure 2, there is still a good range to pick from.

The colour of the walls behind should be considered and often schemes of a restricted colour palette are the

H. crispula with the rare orchid Dactylorhiza elata for a moist shady position.

most effective. A large green hosta underplanted with *Polystichum setiferum* 'Divisilobum' and lily-of-the-valley with a backdrop of variegated green and white ivy creates a cool oasis against a red brick wall. A very simple little bed in the shady corner of two walls could be edged with box and planted with cimicifugas and *H.* 'Fringe Benefit' or with *Digitalis ambigua*, *H.* 'Shade Fanfare' and ferns.

Shady house borders are often the ideal place for a hosta and fern border, the individual plants being selected in relation to the dryness of the soil. Many ferns happily grow with hostas and provide delightful contrasts, so that both groups of plants are visually enhanced.

Fragrant hostas such as *H.* 'Royal Standard', *H.* 'Sugar and Cream', *H.* 'Summer Fragrance', and *H.* 'So Sweet', which form part of the planting shown in Figure 4, should be grown close to doors and windows so that they can be appreciated. Most of the newer scented hostas are happy in partial shade as they flower much earlier than *H. plantaginea*, which must have a very warm spot to flower and is not suitable for colder areas. Smaller-growing daffodils could be planted towards the back of the border, the unfurling shoots of the hostas hiding their leaves as they die down.

Ponds and streams

Hostas look particularly effective near water and although they are not bog plants they will luxuriate just above this level, where their toes are in contact with a constant supply of water and the crowns are above the wet level so that they do not rot off. Many other large-leaved perennials need similar conditions and make excellent companion plants for hostas. The largest is *Gunnera manicata* but in a smaller garden

23

rheums, darmeras (peltiphyllums) or rodgersias could give a similar effect. Tall vertical accents are provided by grasses, sedges, ligularias, filipendulas and moisture-loving irises such as *I. laevigata, I. sibirica* and *I. pseudacorus* (see pages 28–9). Pink and white astilbes with large blue mounds of *H. sieboldiana* 'Elegans' is very effective. Waterside areas need lush planting – massed groups of a limited range of plants is far more effective than many ones or twos, a principle which applies as much to a large lake as to a tiny garden pond.

Most bog plants grow in full sun or partial shade but with a few exceptions the hostas are happier with some shade. Therefore it is better to choose strong-growing varieties and to plant them on the shady side of larger plants so that they will be protected from the intensity of the midday sun. The best hostas for standing up to the sun are the golds and a few green ones. Thick-textured golds such as *H.* 'Sum and Substance' and *H.* 'Midas Touch' will be happy in moist soil in all but the hottest climates but for the rest it is better to give them the filtered light of larger plants above the wettest level of the bog. Green hostas can be particularly good *en masse, H. undulata* 'Erromena',

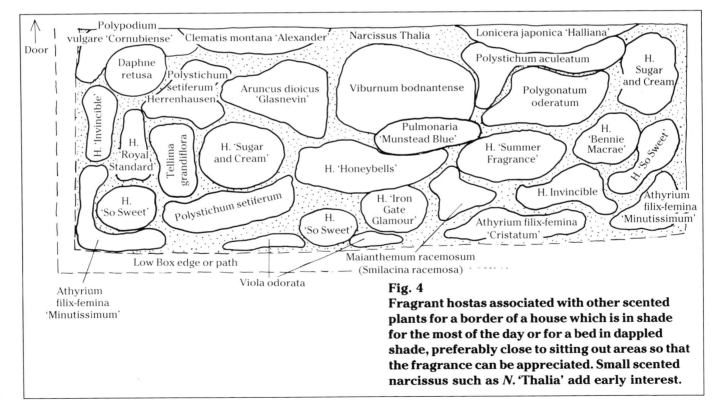

Fig. 4
Fragrant hostas associated with other scented plants for a border of a house which is in shade for the most of the day or for a bed in dappled shade, preferably close to sitting out areas so that the fragrance can be appreciated. Small scented narcissus such as *N.* 'Thalia' add early interest.

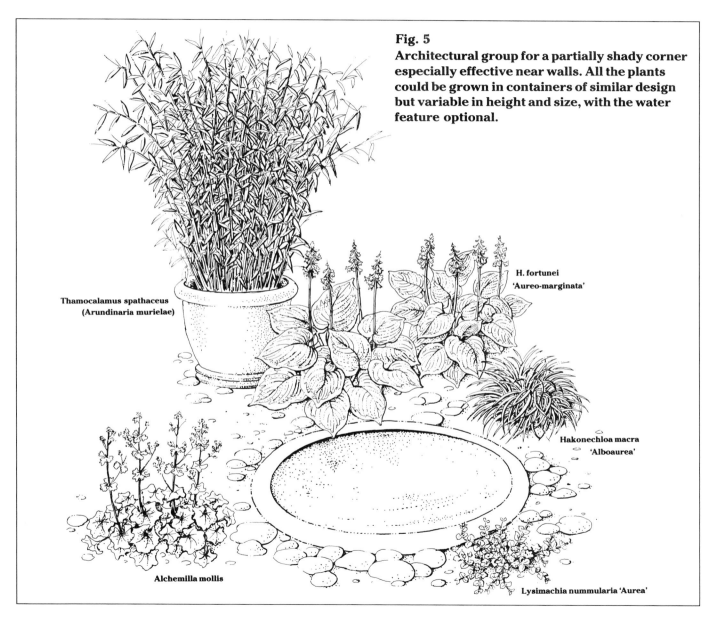

Fig. 5
Architectural group for a partially shady corner especially effective near walls. All the plants could be grown in containers of similar design but variable in height and size, with the water feature optional.

Thamocalamus spathaceus
(Arundinaria murielae)

H. fortunei
'Aureo-marginata'

Hakonechloa macra
'Alboaurea'

Alchemilla mollis

Lysimachia nummularia 'Aurea'

H. 'Tall Boy' and H. montana cooling down the brilliance of day lilies, primulas and astilbes.

Even without the advantage of a natural stream or a pond, there is no need to forgo the pleasure of associating hostas with water in your garden. A small dish filled with water or a large round boulder with a hole drilled in it for a fountain could be the focal point for a simple foliage group (Fig. 5). A bamboo planted in a container to restrict its spread can provide the backdrop to a group of H. fortunei 'Aureo-marginata' underplanted with Alchemilla mollis and the little gold-leaved creeper, Lysimachia nummularia 'Aurea', all mulched with small cobbles to help retain moisture and prevent damage by slugs and snails. Ligularia przewalskii 'The Rocket' could be used instead of the bamboo as long as there is sufficient moisture.

Ground cover

Hostas are very useful under trees and shrubs as ground cover. They make dense clumps or spreading mats and can be left alone for many years. The best types are those with a vigorous habit; stoloniferous hostas are particularly useful for covering large areas. Aesthetically it looks far more effective to use a few varieties in large numbers than a vast medley in ones or twos. For shade and semi-shaded areas hostas are invaluable. They will happily grow where little else will and make excellent ground cover once established. For a balanced effect in the winter useful evergreen ground cover includes ajugas, bergenias, Helleborus foetidus, Iris foetidissima, pulmonarias, tellimas and tiarellas. Hostas that tolerate dry shade are particularly useful as the soil can often be dry under the higher foliage canopy.

Shrub roses can make quite dense canopies and colonies of hostas can exist happily underneath in the dappled shade. The blues are very effective with old roses, and large mounds of H. sieboldiana will hide the bare stems at the base of the roses, while complementing the flowers, especially the mauves, pinks and whites. On a smaller scale drifts of H. 'Halcyon' and hardy geraniums bring cohesion to the rose bed.

One of the most successful uses of hostas as ground cover is in areas of acid soil where they are used extensively under rhododendrons, pieris, camellias and other ericaceous shrubs. They will not only fill the spaces between the shrubs but, with other woodland plants, will extend the season of interest.

Hostas useful for ground cover and mass planting

clausa normalis	'Royal Standard'
fortunei (most)	'Shade Fanfare'
'Francee'	sieboldiana (and forms)
'Fringe Benefit'	sieboldii
'Gold Edger'	'Sugar and Cream'
'Ground Master'	'Sum and Substance'
'Hadspen Blue'	undulata 'Albo-marginata'
'Halcyon'	undulata 'Erromena'
'Honeybells'	undulata 'Univittata'
'Invincible'	ventricosa
lancifolia	'Wide Brim'

Hostas can be left alone to mature and, other than initial establishment, the occasional feed and, if troubled by slugs and snails, the spreading of pellets, they will need no further attention for years.

A damp border in the garden of John Newbold illustrating contrasts in form from Rheum palmatum, Iris pseudacorus 'Variegata' and H. undulata 'Albo-marginata' ('Thomas Hogg').

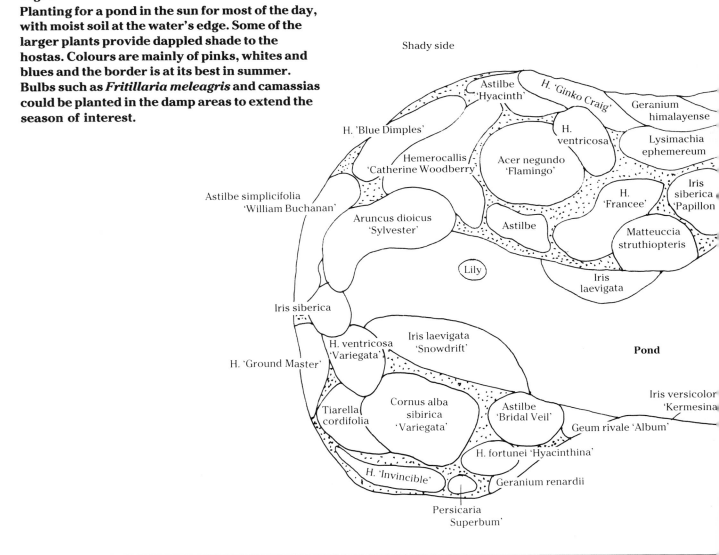

Fig. 6
Planting for a pond in the sun for most of the day, with moist soil at the water's edge. Some of the larger plants provide dappled shade to the hostas. Colours are mainly of pinks, whites and blues and the border is at its best in summer. Bulbs such as *Fritillaria meleagris* and camassias could be planted in the damp areas to extend the season of interest.

Shady side

Astilbe 'Hyacinth'

H. 'Ginko Craig'

Geranium himalayense

H. 'Blue Dimples'

H. ventricosa

Lysimachia ephemereum

Hemerocallis 'Catherine Woodberry'

Acer negundo 'Flamingo'

Iris siberica 'Papillon'

Astilbe simplicifolia 'William Buchanan'

H. 'Francee'

Aruncus dioicus 'Sylvester'

Astilbe

Matteuccia struthiopteris

Lily

Iris laevigata

Iris siberica

Iris laevigata 'Snowdrift'

Pond

H. ventricosa 'Variegata'

H. 'Ground Master'

Iris versicolor 'Kermesina'

Tiarella cordifolia

Cornus alba sibirica 'Variegata'

Astilbe 'Bridal Veil'

Geum rivale 'Album'

H. fortunei 'Hyacinthina'

H. 'Invincible'

Geranium renardii

Persicaria Superbum'

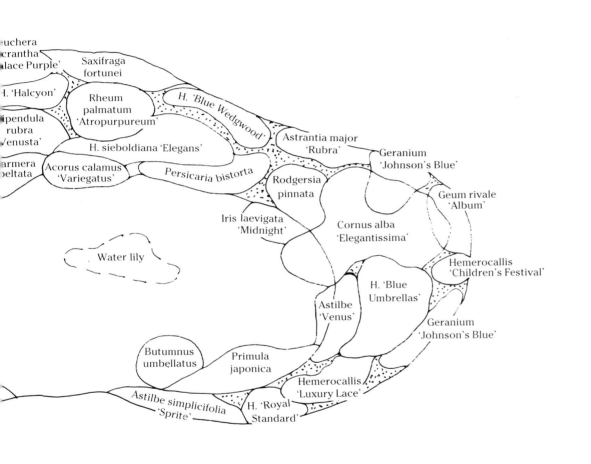

uchera
crantha
lace Purple'

Saxifraga
fortunei

H. 'Halcyon'

Rheum
palmatum
'Atropurpureum'

H. 'Blue Wedgwood'

pendula
rubra
Venusta'

H. sieboldiana 'Elegans'

Astrantia major
'Rubra'

Geranium
'Johnson's Blue'

armera
peltata

Acorus calamus
'Variegatus'

Persicaria bistorta

Rodgersia
pinnata

Geum rivale
'Album'

Iris laevigata
'Midnight'

Cornus alba
'Elegantissima'

Hemerocallis
'Children's Festival'

Water lily

H. 'Blue
Umbrellas'

Astilbe
'Venus'

Geranium
'Johnson's Blue'

Butumnus
umbellatus

Primula
japonica

Hemerocallis
'Luxury Lace'

Astilbe simplicifolia
'Sprite'

H. 'Royal
Standard'

Sunnier side

29

Alpine beds

The shady parts of rock gardens and raised beds make excellent sites for many of the smaller-growing and often not very vigorous hostas. Most would be completely lost in the larger border and need to be seen in closer proximity for the beauty of their leaves and flowers to be appreciated. Alpine beds are often covered in chippings and this can help to give a cool root run and reduce the problem of slugs and snails. They generally need a fair amount of shade and will often grow happily in a rocky crevice where they can look particularly effective. Most need to be established in pots and with the very small ones it is advisable to keep a piece growing in a pot to guard against loss, whether from slugs, unseasonal weather or accidental removal in winter when weeding.

Small ferns, hepaticas, mossy saxifrages, cyclamens, erythroniums, trilliums and a host of other shade-loving alpines are complemented by the addition of hostas, the choice being determined by the degree of moisture in the soil.

Smaller hostas generally under 25 cm (10 in) in height

'Amanuma'
'Blond Elf'
'Blue Blush'
'Blue Moon'
'Blue Skies'
'Carrie Ann'
'Celebration'

A fragrant group suitable for a partially shady house border. _H._ 'So Sweet' (white flowers) and _H._ 'Iron Gate Glamour' with ferns and _Pachysandra terminalis_ 'Green Carpet'.

'Chartreuse Wiggles'
'Dawn' ('Sunset') (see 'Hydon Sunset'*)
'Dorset Blue'
'Duchess'
'Elfin Power'
'Fresh'
'Ginko Craig'
'Goldbrook Grace'
'Golden Prayers'
'Green with Envy' (see 'Hydon Sunset'*)
'Hadspen Heron'
'Hakujima' (see 'Saishu Jima'*)
'Harmony'
'Hydon Sunset'
'Lemon Lime'
'Little Aurora' (see 'Golden Prayers'*)
'Little White Lines'
minor
'Pixie Power' (see 'Elfin Power'*)
'Royalty'
'Saishu Jima'
'Shining Tot'
sieboldii (most forms)
'Squiggles' (see _H. sieboldii_ 'Shiro-kabitan'*)
tardiflora
'Thumb Nail' (see _H. venusta_*)
'Tiny Tears'
'Vanilla Cream'
venusta
venusta 'Variegated'

* in Chapter 6

CHAPTER 3

The Importance of Colour in Garden Design

The more subdued palette is far more effective in creating areas of tranquillity; part of a garden or a border can be planted in individual colour schemes to achieve this. The white garden is in fashion at the moment, often in a separate enclosure delineated by yew hedges to intensify the paleness of the flowers. A blue scheme allows the eye to recede, making a garden seem larger, whereas red immediately draws the eye – a red border is exciting but not tranquil.

The main quality of most foliage plants is that they are restful and create peaceful gardens. Hostas are not brash plants and generally look far more effective when planted within a scheme using a limited colour range, although the plainer-leaved ones are valuable in toning down fussy borders and bringing discipline into the garden.

Different colour schemes can be used in the same area by planting for a winter and summer effect, the bright spring garden of hellebores, pulmonarias and bulbs becoming a cool oasis of greens and creams when the light of the summer becomes more intense. The subdued light of a low sun is totally different from the harsher effect of the midsummer rays, and canopies of summer foliage will soften and filter. Colour varies from season to season, day to day, hour by hour and even from person to person: colour is a subjective thing. The interplay of light on hosta foliage changes with the texture or colour of the plant, and some colours work far better with each other – the greys and blues with shades of pink, and whites or yellow with blues and white.

USING VARIEGATED LEAVES

Many hostas have variegated leaves, the edges can be green, blue, yellow, cream or white, the centres the same colours and they can be in nearly every combination. If you need a gold centre with a green margin, H. 'Gold Standard' or H. 'September Sun' would be suitable, if a blue edged in creamy yellow is required, then H. 'Frances Williams' would be perfect.

Variegated leaves are dominant and must be used with care; they need plain neighbours or those that echo the colour scheme. Too much variegation gives a jumbled up hodge podge, the eye does not know where to focus, but a single green and white hosta rising from a mass of filigree ferns is restful. Sometimes within a limited spectrum variegation used in different scales is very effective. Try H. undulata 'Albo-marginata' (H. 'Thomas Hogg') against Euonymus fortunei 'Emerald Gaiety', the larger leaf of the hosta echoed by the much smaller leaf of the shrub. This contrast in size or shape is very important when mixing variegated plants together. A backdrop of gold-edged ivy leaves clothing a wall would be complemented by a hosta with gold variegation but not by H. 'Francee' which has a very crisp white edge.

White variegated hostas are best not used with yellow or yellow-variegated ones as the whole effect is dissipated, although schemes using hostas which are yellow edged in spring, then cream- or white-edged later, can be devised, the yellow tones echoing the spring garden and the whiter ones the summer effect.

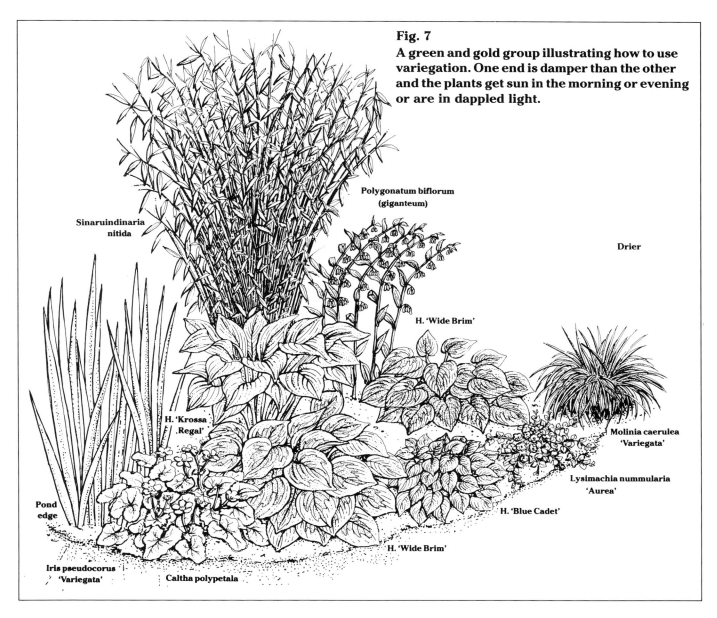

Fig. 7
A green and gold group illustrating how to use variegation. One end is damper than the other and the plants get sun in the morning or evening or are in dappled light.

Polygonatum biflorum
(giganteum)

Sinaruindinaria
nitida

Drier

H. 'Wide Brim'

H. 'Krossa
Regal'

Molinia caerulea
'Variegata'

Pond
edge

Lysimachia nummularia
'Aurea'

H. 'Blue Cadet'

H. 'Wide Brim'

Iris pseudocorus
'Variegata'

Caltha polypetala

It is the hosta that has strong white variegation all season that needs some plain neighbours and to be associated with plants that have white, not yellow variegation.

Variegated plants are not a panacea for interesting gardens. Used carefully they make focal points and can look very effective but used indiscriminately they often look a mess. White flowers with white variegation or yellow spires with gold variegation are complementary: *Ligularia prewalckii* 'The Rocket' planted with *H. fortunei* 'Aureo-marginata' and *Iris pseudacorus* 'Variegata' is a very dramatic and successful group. In summer the tall, black-stemmed yellow spires of the ligularia intensify the gold margin on the hosta as the gold stripes of the iris are beginning to fade to green. Earlier, the most dominant plant would have been the iris, its vividly striped gold and green leaves seen against the cut-leaved mound of the green ligularia and the rounded form of the hosta. A far more subtle effect is *Aruncus dioicus* 'Glasnevin' planted with *H.* 'Sugar and Cream'. The green of both plants leans towards the yellow, the flowering spires of the aruncus are not pure white but have creamy undertones as does the margin of the hosta, so both plants complement each other perfectly.

Figure 7 is an example of how to use variegated plants and it would be equally suitable for a border with a gold and green theme. The bed is in partial shade, one end bordering a pond or with an area of boggy soil which is planted with *Iris pseudacorus* 'Variegata' and *Caltha polypetala*, the plain green round leaves perfectly accentuating the iris. *H.* 'Wide Brim' with creamy gold bands has very similar varieg-

A superb clump of *H. sieboldiana* 'Elegans' with lush moisture-loving perennials in the garden of Derek Fox in Essex.

ation to the iris but in a completely different leaf form and it also has plain neighbours, the vase-shaped *H.* 'Krossa Regal', the arching bamboo and, for earlier interest, the giant Solomon's seal bedecked with bells of greeny white flowers and a similar habit, but on a smaller scale, to the bamboo. As the season advances the creamy yellow edge of the hosta becomes lighter, accentuating the striped cream and green leaves of the molinia and setting off its airy panicles to perfection.

Although molinias are usually grown in full sun, they are perfectly happy in dappled light as long as they get sun for part of the day and, like hostas, they do better in fertile soil. Their variegation is particularly effective with a range of variegated hostas that have creamy yellow margins such as *H.* 'Shade Fanfare' and *H. fluctuans* 'Variegated'.

White gardens

Hostas with white in their foliage grow far better in the shade, and therefore even in quite dark corners a lightening effect can be created. They will usually flower sparsely so that even the purist will have few flower stems to cut off if they are of the wrong tone. Some hostas have white flowers but when designing with them it is the colour of the foliage that must be of prime importance: a large gold mound with white blooms would be discordant in a green and white or grey and white scheme, whereas *H.* 'Francee', which is not white flowering but has excellent green and white foliage, would look far more effective in such a scheme. Blue-grey foliage is often part of a white garden and therefore most blue hostas are useful; some even have white flowers.

Even within white gardens there are subtle tones of other colours – few white flowers are paper white;

most have tints of yellow, pink or blue and hostas can be selected to pick up the different shades, using blue foliage with lavender and pinky tones or greens and creams with the yellow-tinged whites. In shadier places hostas are invaluable; they are the ideal companions for a wide range of white-flowering perennials such as *Dicentra spectabilis* 'Alba', *Pulmonaria* 'Sissinghurst White', *Astrantia major* 'Shaggy', *Polygonatum falcatum* 'Variegatum' and *Chelone obliqua* 'Alba' to name but a few. When well grown, *H. crispula*, with its lovely undulating white-margined,

green leaves planted with Solomon's seal and lily-of-the-valley is a picture. *Miscanthus sinsensis* 'Variegatus', with its green and white arching foliage, *Iris foetidissima* 'Variegata' and *Iris foetidissima* 'Fructo-alba' bedecked in autumn with delightful white fruit, could be added to provide invaluable vertical accents. *H.* 'Snowden' and the scented *H.* 'Royal Standard' are two of the best of the white-flowering hostas to plant in drifts.

Figure 8 is a very simple but effective white and green foliage scheme in a shady corner. A small group

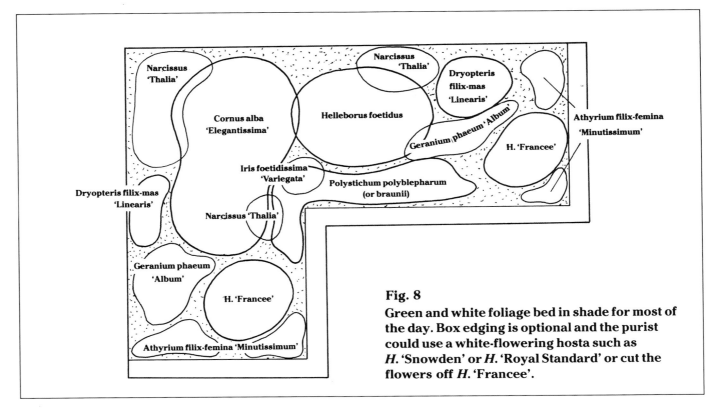

Fig. 8
Green and white foliage bed in shade for most of the day. Box edging is optional and the purist could use a white-flowering hosta such as *H.* 'Snowden' or *H.* 'Royal Standard' or cut the flowers off *H.* 'Francee'.

of *Cornus alba* 'Elegantissima' is underplanted with *Helleborus foetidus*, the red stems of the shrub contrasting with the red rims of the flowers of the hellebore in early spring. *Narcissus* 'Thalia', a delightful fragrant daffodil, flowers just as the leaves of the hostas are starting to emerge, *H.* 'Francee' has pronounced reddish shoots on emergence and as the cornus becomes covered in green and white leaves, the hosta pushes up its foliage mound of green and white. The ferns give contrasts in leaf form and *Geranium phaeum album* carries light airy white flowers in summer.

White- or near white-flowered hostas suitable for a white garden

'Blue Angel'
'Blue Seer' (see *H. sieboldiana* 'Elegans'*)
'Carrie Ann'
'Emerald Isle' (see *H. sieboldii**)
kikutii 'Pruinose'
'Louisa' (see *H.* sieboldii*)
'Love Pat'
'Osprey'
plantaginea
'Royal Standard'
'Sea Lotus Leaf'
sieboldiana (some)
sieboldii 'Alba'
'Snow Cap'
'Snowden'
'Snowflakes' (see *H. sieboldii* 'Alba'*)
'So Sweet'
'Sugar and Cream'
tokudama

* in Chapter 6

Green gardens

There are many different shades of green: *H. montana* has large shiny leaves, *H.* 'Black Hills' comes with very dark, seersuckered foliage and *H.* 'Jade Scepter' is a pale chartreuse. A predominantly green foliage scheme relies on contrasts of leaf form for the different effects, and vertical accents from plants such as day lilies, irises and grasses are very important. Leaves will dominate the scheme although flowers are perfectly acceptable. Green borders can be very restful, especially near buildings or in shady corners. Bricks, paving cobbles and wood are complemented by the simplicity of a green scheme but the foliage must be interesting.

The summer effect could include hostas, alchemillas, ferns, ligularias, bamboos and grasses with evergreen effects from *Itea ilicifolia*, *Osmanthus heterophyllus*, *Viburnum tinus*, hellebores, liriopes, pachysandras and sarcococcas. If the soil is acid rhododendrons, camellias and *Trochodendron aralioides* will also flourish. Many of these plants have greenish flowers and this can further exploit the green theme.

Imagine a backdrop of *Garrya elliptica*, *Hedera colchica* 'Paddy's Pride' and *Hydrangea petiolaris*, with evergreen interest from *Daphne laureola*, *Helleborus corsicus*, green and white shades of *Helleborus orientalis* and the shiny green foliage of *Iris foetidissima*. The green stems of *Cornus stolonifera* 'Flavirama' could be underplanted with *Narcissus cyclamineus* 'Jenny' and *H. fortunei* 'Aureo-marginata'. *Liriope muscari*, *Ajuga reptans* 'Alba', mitellas, asarums and smaller-growing bergenias would serve to clothe the spaces between the smaller hostas. *Dryopteris filix-mas* 'Linearis', with its slender, erect, finely cut fronds and *Digitalis lutea*, a perennial foxglove with small creamy yellow flowers, would be the perfect foil to the hostas. The border is subdued, an oasis of green.

Gold gardens

The best-known gold-leaved hosta is *H. fortunei* 'Aurea' which, although yellow in spring, fades to green with maturity. Most of the newer gold hostas stay gold all season. They need some sun to colour but not too much – dappled light is ideal. Without any protection they will scorch and become papery white, while in too much shade they will turn chartreuse. Sometimes this colour is very useful in deep shade as it gives a lightening effect and gold hostas can be planted in shade to achieve it. As a general rule the thicker the leaf then the more sun they need to colour. *H.* 'Sum and Substance', *H.* 'Midas Touch', *H.* 'Gold Edger', *H.* 'Golden Medallion' and *H.* 'Gold Regal' will all grow in sunny spots, in all but the hottest climates as long as the site is moist, but *H.* 'Piedmont Gold' with its thinner leaf texture must have some shade.

A border of only gold hostas would be monotonous but used with green and green and gold variegation they can be effective. There are many yellow-flowering plants that associate with hostas, particularly hemerocallis, ligularias, alchemillas, and some irises. Figure 9 is a scheme for a moist bed in dappled shade, perhaps on the edge of a pond, or the planting could be adapted to a formal design for a courtyard garden. Most of the plants except for the hostas will also grow in sun as long as the soil is damp and this can be exploited by planting the hostas on the shady side of the *Ligularia przewalskii* 'The Rocket' and the *Miscanthus sinensis* 'Zebrinus'. *Cortaderia selloana* 'Gold Band' would be equally effective although it needs more sun than the miscanthus.

The ligularia has an excellent mound of large, round, serrated green leaves and in late summer very tall black stems carry bright yellow flowers, a dramatic accent plant in a bog garden or near a formal pond in a modern setting, perhaps mulched with large cobbles. It is the perfect foil to *H.* 'Gold Standard', which needs some shade so that it does not scorch but if the light is too poor it will not colour. *Alchemilla mollis*, an invaluable plant with rounded velvety leaves, on a smaller scale than the ligularia, has sprays of lime green flowers for weeks in midsummer. Its tendency to self seed can be exploited, letting it weave in and out of the border. The graceful mound of the miscanthus has the gold bands on its narrow green leaves emphasized by the two gold hostas. In a formal scheme these could be planted as a separate group with alchemillas and day lilies and covered in cobbles. Golden daffodils and winter aconites would provide early interest.

A mixed planting of green and gold would be effective for a bed which has sun in the morning or the evening. *Cornus alba* 'Aurea', *Iris foetidissima* and *Bergenia* 'Bressingham White' would all provide winter interest before the hostas emerge in the spring. *H.* 'Sum and Substance', a strong architectural mound could be used as a specimen. Other large, gold hostas could include *H.* 'Sea Gold Star', H. 'Midas Touch' and *H.* 'Zounds'. (*H. tokudama* 'Aureo-nebulosa' and *H.* 'Frances Williams' could be included but it is important that the variegation should not be dominant.) *H.* 'Golden Prayers', *H.* 'Gold Edger' and *H.* 'Hydon Sunset' would all contribute as edgers and gound cover. *Alchemilla xanthochlora*, greener and smaller growing than *A. mollis*, would contrast perfectly with *H.* 'Chinese Sunrise' while the slight green tone inside the white border of *H.* 'Moonlight' could be accented by the dark, glossy fronds of *Polystichum braunii*.

H. 'Gold Standard', excellent in the garden and in a pot. It should be positioned so that it receives just enough sun to colour, but not enough to scorch.

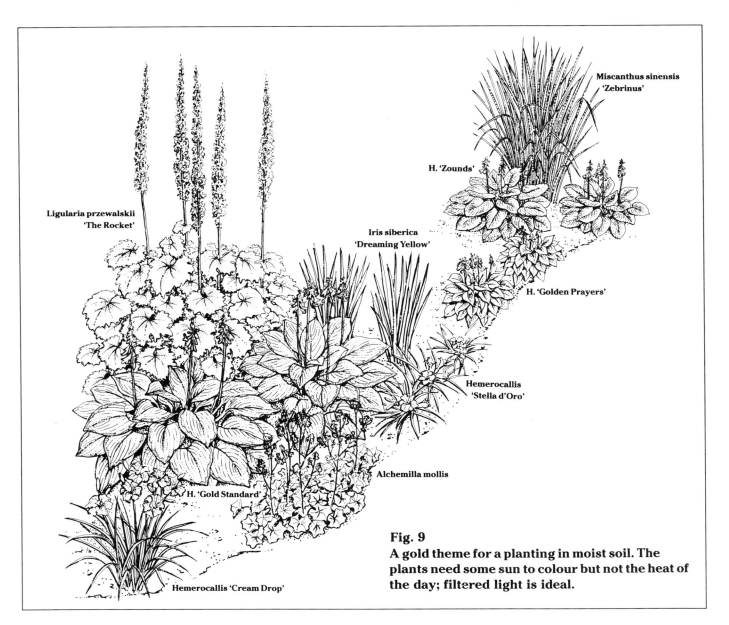

Miscanthus sinensis
'Zebrinus'

H. 'Zounds'

Ligularia przewalskii
'The Rocket'

Iris siberica
'Dreaming Yellow'

H. 'Golden Prayers'

Hemerocallis
'Stella d'Oro'

Alchemilla mollis

H. 'Gold Standard'

Hemerocallis 'Cream Drop'

Fig. 9
**A gold theme for a planting in moist soil. The
plants need some sun to colour but not the heat of
the day; filtered light is ideal.**

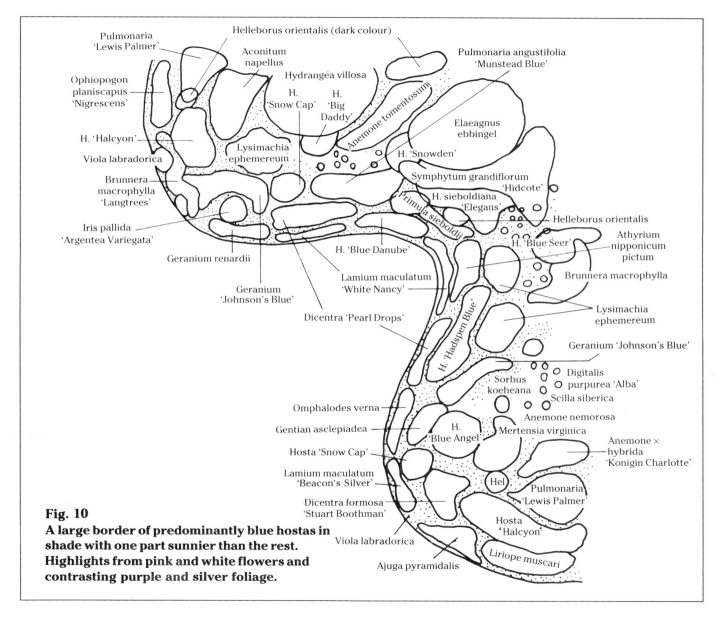

Fig. 10
A large border of predominantly blue hostas in shade with one part sunnier than the rest. Highlights from pink and white flowers and contrasting purple and silver foliage.

Blue gardens

There are many excellent blue-foliaged hostas, but they need to grow in partial or full shade to maintain their colour. Planted in full sun they will be green by the end of the season as the surface coating on the leaf will have disappeared. In cool areas blue hostas will often retain their colour to the end of the season and the hotter the climate the more shade they will need to stay blue. The choice of plain blue hostas is wide-ranging, but those with variegation are as yet few. The best known is *H.* 'Frances Williams' but others to look out for include *H. tokudama* 'Aureo-nebulosa', *H.* 'Regal Splendor', *H.* 'Snow Cap', and *H.* 'Pizzazz'.

The effect of blue foliage is rather different from a blue sunny border where flowers predominate and the composition is tempered by airy flowers and spires. Blue foliage needs contrasts in colour such as *H.* 'Halcyon' planted with *Heuchera micrantha* 'Palace Purple' and *Ajuga pyramidalis* 'Metallica Crispa' or contrast in form such as from *Liriope muscari*, the blue flower spikes and strappy leaves perfectly set off by the rounded mounds of the hostas. *Lysimachia ephemereum*, not always the easiest plant to place, reveals its refined beauty in association with blue hostas and with *Athyrium niponicum pictum*, its lacy fronds tinged with greys and purples. Whites, pinks, lilacs and purples lighten the effect as do golds and whites in a blue-gold scheme.

In Figure 10 *Elaeagnus ebbingei* provides an evergreen silvery green backdrop, while the bluish-tinged pinnate leaves of the sorbus and the hydrangea's felted greyish foliage complement the lower level. The spring-flowering perennials such as pulmonarias, hellebores and scillas as well as those for the later season such as aconitums are planted towards the back of the border. Blue-foliaged hostas, white foxgloves and lilies dominate the summer scene. Ideally this type of planting needs to be able to be viewed from a distance, the blues and whites in a glade of evergreen shrubs and deciduous trees, against a shady wall covered in greenery or a yew hedge. Many of the plants are allowed to intermingle, dicentras skirting the unfurling leaves of the hostas and as they die down the willow gentian (*Gentiana asclepiadea*), aconitums and *Anemone tomentosa* 'Robustissima' take their place.

The spring garden could be further enlivened by golden daffodils and often the most successful effects are achieved by an early blue and gold garden giving way to blues, purples, pinks and white. Schemes with blue need fine tuning as the effect of light can intensify or dissipate the many shades. Some blues look wonderful together and others do not work at all. The inclusion of flowers of different hues and generous groups of hostas will usually bring cohesion, the hostas acting as foils and links to any discordant elements among the other plants.

**Complete ground cover, the blueness of
H. 'Halcyon' intensified by the green and gold.**

CHAPTER 4

The Use of Hostas as Container Plants

Most hostas make superb pot plants, complementing a wide range of ornamental containers. I have been growing considerable numbers of specimen hostas in containers for many years, mainly for exhibiting, and have developed a love-hate relationship with a few of them. Some grow better in pots than in the garden but others are certainly a problem to maintain after the first four or five years.

Great care should go not only into the selection of the hosta but into the container and the position in the garden. Regardless of the ornamental container used it is far easier to grow a hosta in a plastic pot of a size relevant to the growth of the plant, and to put this inside a decorative container, with cobbles or some other medium placed over the pot to hide the inner container. In winter the hosta can be removed and something more interesting put in its place. If repotting or other care is required this is much easier to carry out from a cheap plastic pot than trying to remove a specimen from what could be a very valuable container.

Ideally the hosta needs to be in a place out of the wind and not in the heat of the sun; early morning or evening sun is far less damaging and some even need it to colour. A solitary pot is more prone to the elements as it does not have the protection of neighbouring plants. Containers can be placed anywhere in the garden, but tend to be near the house as this simplifies watering.

Hostas with cascading mounds are particularly effective and can often stand alone or as a pair to emphasize a particular feature. *H.* 'Green Fountain' looks very elegant, its shape shown off to perfection in a pot, but it needs plenty of room or will be easily damaged. Others need to be placed in groups, each plant carefully chosen to set off its neighbour. The backdrop should always be considered as part of the scheme. *H.* 'Gold Standard' will make a superb specimen in a large container. Green on unfurling and brilliant gold with a green rim if given dappled light later on in the season, it could look spectacular placed against a green background or dark coloured brick walls. But near a pink colour-washed wall it would be horrendous; far better to use a plain green or blue variety in this situation – *H.* 'Snowden', with large grey-green leaves and lovely white flowers would not be out of place and it seems to grow better in a large container than in the ground.

Variegated hostas need the same care in placing as they do in the garden. The easiest are those with white variegation – *H.* 'Francee' grows very well in a container and will look good against most backgrounds – but green and yellow or blue and yellow variegation need far more thought. Generally it is better to have only one variety in a pot and if it is felt that the container is large enough for other plants to be included then these must be chosen with care. Small ferns, creeping Jenny, periwinkles or trailing ivies will all complement the hosta.

Gold hostas are not the easiest to place and some do not grow well in pots other than in the short term. *H.* 'Sum and Substance', with enormous chartreuse-gold leaves like dinner plates, could look sumptuous against a bamboo in a corner that gets some sun as long as the container is simple and of large dimensions.

Town gardens often have shady corners or even areas where no sun penetrates; the soil if there is any, is often very poor and the only satisfactory way to grow plants is in containers. They may range from tiny pots to large raised beds. Hostas are the ideal plants for these gardens, especially in association with other shade-loving plants such as ferns, bamboos, cut-leaf acers, and large-leaved evergreens. The most popular container hosta in Japan is *H. fluctuans* 'Variegated', still rare in the west but spectacular in a large round glazed pot, an excellent focal point in a courtyard.

Containers do not have to be limited to pots: special planters made from brick, railway sleepers or timber can be an integral part of a terrace area. These should be treated the same way as a small border and are only suitable for hostas if in shade for the hottest part of the day. On a much smaller scale a deep stone sink is suitable for the tiny hostas.

When the area to plant is small a careful choice of the plant material and containers must be made. Containers need to be balanced not only with the hostas but with each other. Containers can soften modern architecture and, when used with discretion, complement period buildings, but too many styles and different materials filled with a medley of plants is just as lacking in cohesion as a similar planting in the garden.

Effective little groups can be made by standing the pots on cobbles or by incorporating small water features such as that shown in Fig. 5. (page 25). Fragrant varieties such as *H.* 'Summer Fragrance', *H.* 'So Sweet', *H.* 'Invincible', and *H.* 'Sugar and Cream' grow particularly well in large containers and if placed near sitting out areas, the air will be deliciously scented in late summer when they come into bloom.

Hostas in containers are far more demanding of regular attention than in the ground (see next chapter for cultivation advice) but this can pay dividends especially in early years, when a suitable pot-grown plant will grow far better than one of a similar size planted in the ground. Nearly all except those with *H. sieboldiana* and *H. tokudama* in their parentage grow well in pots.

The following hostas are particularly recommended for pots, some growing better in a container than in the ground.

fortunei (all)	*lancifolia* (and forms)
'Francee'	*minor*
'Goldbrook'	*nakaiana* (and related
'Gold Standard'	hybrids)
'Golden Prayers'	'Reversed'
'Golden Tiara'	*sieboldii* (and related
'Green Fountain'	hybrids)
'Halcyon'	'Snowden'
'Hydon Sunset'	'So Sweet'
'Invincible'	'Summer Fragrance'
kikutii (and forms)	*undulata* (all)
'Krossa Regal'	

Hostas for flower arrangers

Most hostas are useful in flower arrangements, but some are better than others, as very thin leaves are hard to condition and do not last as long in water. The choice is wide but for a basic collection most arrangers like a variety of leaf sizes and colours. Many grow their plants in pots as it is certainly easier to be sure of a supply of undamaged leaves, so necessary for floral work.

The same principles of colour, shape and texture apply in an arrangement as in the garden. It is usually

45

better to use the foliage of one hosta variety than many different ones, and the simplicity of the leaf is an excellent foil to frilly flowers.

All parts of a hosta can be used, the leaves, flowers and seed heads, although to most arrangers it is the foliage that is of paramount importance. It always better to pick material early in the morning or late in the evening and to immerse the stems, cut on the slant, in water placed in a cool place until they are needed. The leaves can even be completely immersed in water for short periods without coming to any harm. Flowers and seeds heads can also be dried or preserved in silica gel. Some, such as *H.* 'Christmas Tree', have black seed pods and others, such as *H.* 'Celebration', are red; these could also be varnished for winter arrangements.

Hostas described in Chapter 6 which are particularly suitable for floral work are marked with an asterisk (although not all are yet readily available).

A white garden group on the stand of Goldbrook Plants at Chelsea 1991. *H.* **'Gloriosa' (with the narrow white edge) and** *H.* **'Ginko Craig' the perfect complement for** *Zantedeschia aethiopica* **'Crowborough'.**

CHAPTER 5

Cultivation

In the garden

In earlier chapters we have looked at the requirements of shade and moisture for hostas when grown to
perfection. Hostas grown in less than ideal conditions
can still make satisfactory garden plants, but some
effort is amply repaid. Once a strong root system is
established, many hostas will stand a surprising
amount of neglect. They are long-lived, relatively easy
to cultivate and can be left undivided for many years.

PLANTING OUT

Hostas are dormant in the winter and although they
can be moved and planted nearly all the year round as
long as care is taken, the ideal time is in the spring
when the new shoots are about to emerge and new
roots will quickly establish as the soil warms up.
Planting in autumn in moist soil before the advent of
frosts is successful with strong vigorous divisions, but
not to be recommended for those that need more
attention to establish themselves well. It is far better to
leave these in a greenhouse or cold frame so that they
do not become frosted and rot off.

Pot-grown plants are often easier to establish and
the effort of potting on new divisions, especially if very
small, and giving them optimum care for a year or two
can result in far better plants in a shorter time. Very
small-growing hostas and those that are highly
variegated and lack chlorophyll, especially if expensive, should always be grown on for a year or two.

Hostas bought in pots can be planted all through the
summer months as long as they are kept watered. The
advantage of doing this is that because they are
planted in leaf they are more likely to be in the right
place in the scheme and the effect is immediate. Once
planted they should be left alone to mature. It takes
time for the mature leaf form to develop and constant
splitting up or disturbance means that some gardeners
never appreciate the beauty of a mature clump.

SOILS AND SITES

Hostas prefer free-draining but moisture-retentive soil
with adequate organic matter. The most difficult soils
are those that are sandy or solid clay; the ideal is a rich
loam. Neutral to slightly acidic soils result in the most
luxuriant leaf colour, especially for green- and blue-
leaved hostas, but as long as the soil is not thin,
overlying chalk, hostas will grow happily in limey
soils. Sandy soils need an abundance of organic matter
to be added and clay benefits from being opened up to
improve the drainage; digging in pea shingle and
adding manure will in time result in a very satisfactory
planting medium for hostas as clay soils are usually
fertile and once the roots are established sufficient
moisture is usually available.

Peaty loams or even free-draining raised beds which
have adequate moisture and are not in the baking sun
make ideal homes for many of the smaller and often
stoloniferous hostas.

Large, strong-growing hostas need more soil
preparation than tiny varieties. The planting hole
should relate in size to the vigour of the hosta, and an
adequate provision of manure or compost added. The
newly planted hosta does not want to come into direct
contact with the organic matter as too much feed
before the plant has grown can result in brown, soft
leaves and even death if the cell structure is destroyed.
Organic matter is best placed in the bottom of the hole

with a layer of loam, leaf mould or a proprietary compost placed over it. If the hosta is an open-ground division then it should be spread over a slight mound, the roots spread out with the crown near the surface and firmed in.

If planting from a container, freeing some of the roots, especially if curling round in the pot, helps establishment. A slight mound is not required but firming in is important. It should be planted at the same level as in the container. After watering in, mulching will help to retain moisture and in the first season of growth it is important that the plant continues to have adequate moisture. Drooping leaves tell their own story but young plants do not want to be drowned.

Failing a supply of organic matter hostas can be planted in good quality compost, ideally one that has a rough structure, and fed on a great variety of fertilizers and foliar feeds. It is best to remove flower scapes from young plants so that all the plant's energy can go into making a good root system.

FEEDING

Hostas grow much faster if they are fed and watered regularly. Feeding in the early days should be little and often, such as a fortnightly feed of Phostrogen at half strength or, if in areas of limey water, a liquid feed containing iron. A very easy way to make sure the plant has adequate feed is to incorporate slow-release pellets in the compost in the planting hole, but never exceed the stated dose – very few pellets are required. It is better to use less than the recommended dosage as too much feed to very young plants can be harmful. When established, especially if the hosta is large and vigorous, a mulch of well-rotted manure or compost in the autumn will be appreciated, but not over the crown which is better protected with a layer of bark or peat. The smaller the hosta the less food and water it requires, but general conditions become more important. *H. sieboldiana* forms will happily grow in clay soils as long as the planting site is well-prepared, but the much smaller *H. venusta* would probably turn up its toes and die.

Growing in containers

Cultivation of hostas in containers is slightly different from in the open ground, although some of the same principles apply. A newly acquired division or a small container-grown hosta must not be placed in an enormous pot as the closed environment of the container can often result in failure. Any container can be used as the final home as long as it is not shallow, drains well – root rot can cause just as many problems as a failure to water – and the planting medium it contains is open in structure, to allow the roots oxygen as well as water and nutrients.

PLANTING UP AND POTTING ON

A proprietary coarse, peat-based compost containing 25% grit and slightly acidic is ideal, but home-made mixtures of rich loam mixed with peat, bark or leaf mould to which 25% grit or perlite has been added can be satisfactory as long as a feeding routine is followed. Up to a third of very old horse manure or garden compost can also be used in the formulation but it must be old and not fresh. The easiest way to feed is to incorporate slow-release pellets into the compost as the fertilizer is activated by water and warmth, the plant taking up the amounts it requires as it grows. Slow-release pellets need to be applied every spring but do not give more than the recommended dosage. Any additional feeding can be given in liquid form when watering, which should be into the compost and not on to the hosta leaves as these will mark.

If the compost is slightly lower than the top of the

pot, it is much easier to give a thorough soaking every other day or so. The compost should be moist but not saturated, and although rain will help to keep the leaves clean in periods of drought great care must be taken with overhead watering. It must be done when the sun is not out or there will be scorch damage; droplets of water on the leaves act like magnifying glasses and cause unsightly brown spots. Glaucous foliage suffers the most from watermarks, especially if the water is limey and it is not possible to remove the lime deposits without removing the surface bloom. If the water used is limey it may be necessary to counteract this by using products with extra iron in order that the compost does not become too alkaline. The health of the plant is not really affected, only its visual appearance, and the leaves, especially green ones, become rather pale.

CONTAINERS

It is far easier to keep a hosta happy in a plastic pot as these retain moisture, and in the growing season it is very important that the container does not dry out; in a terracotta pot failure to water results in the porous pot taking the moisture out of the hosta's root system. If a large clump is to be planted in a container then the pot must obviously be of adequate size, but most people start with a newly acquired, relatively small plant, and this will grow much better if it is potted on in stages, rather than put in a large pot straight away.

This does not mean you cannot use that large decorative pot you want to place strategically in your garden, but you may need to place a smaller pot inside it for a year or so, and when the plant is nearly filling this with roots, move up to a larger size. This pot-within-a-pot arrangement may be the best of both worlds if a favoured decorative pot is of terracotta or other porous material, since as well as hiding a less attractive plastic pot, it also gives the hosta roots a non-porous home which will not leach precious moisture from them. Having a container within a container, with shingle or a similar medium filling the gap between the two also helps to create a humid environment and acts as a deterrent to slug and snail damage. A further advantage is that in winter it is very easy to lift out the hosta and use something in its place while the hosta is dormant. The hosta can be placed in a cold-frame, unheated garage or shed and nearly forgotten about until spring as it needs very little water and is best kept on the dry side, but it should not be allowed to dry out to the extent that the compost shrinks from the sides of the pot.

In areas of extreme frosts, hostas are often grown in containers which are planted in the ground and then removed to protected areas in the winter. It is very important that water does not come into direct contact with the crown of the containerized hosta when it is in the frozen state and some form of protection must be given such as a mulch and covering with plastic or frost cloth or it must be buried in the ground.

It is best not to place containers in too hot a position as they can rapidly heat up in summer and in extreme cases root damage can occur. The pot inside a pot should help to prevent this.

Potting on is best done in the spring and, if the plant has become pot-bound, root pruning will encourage new, younger feeding roots. Tip the plant out of the pot, lay it on its side and, with a sharp knife – a carving knife is ideal – cut a thin slice off the bottom. Unravel some of the stronger-growing roots and repot in new compost. As long as the knife is clean there should be no infection but a sound precaution is to clean the knife between dealing with each plant.

DIAGNOSING PROBLEMS

Most hostas reach maturity after four or five years and even if the pot is large problems can develop with

49

some varieties. Some hostas exhibit problems at a much earlier age than others and even in the same variety in the same sized container, given exactly the same cultural care, one can develop problems before another. Most hostas are perfectly happy in a large pot for a considerable number of years – in fact, some seem to grow better in pots. Observations from growing hostas for exhibiting over the past nine years indicate there is a general pattern but there will always be exceptions to the rule.

If your hosta appears to be late in emergence (remembering not all hostas come up at the same time) and the leaves appear small, possibly deformed, then it is time to investigate the root system. Take a knife and cut the rootstock in half, and you will probably find a very congested, hard root core. There will probably be two tiers of roots, the individual crowns are no longer able to make roots into the compost and if the divisions are pulled apart you will find under the crown a thick mass that is very hard and woody. Such a plant, if left alone, will just deteriorate and finally die, but if split up and repotted or the individual pieces planted in the garden, some, though probably not all, will recover and develop into healthy new plants. Root congestion like this can also happen in the ground if plants are neglected, although it is less common.

Sometimes part of the plant seems to be growing properly but the odd crown has leaves that are smaller and twisted, and if this plant is cut up as soon as is practical (it can be done in a greenhouse when the plant is growing), virtually all the individual pieces will recover and after a season or so return to normal.

If the roots have rotted off this again can indicate that the crowns are congested but also may be caused by other problems such as pests and diseases. When dealing with the individual pieces it is important to remove any damage and cut away any rot. A dose of fungicide can be beneficial before repotting.

Very strong-growing hostas are the most difficult to grow long term in containers; they will never reach full maturity of leaf and they will always be smaller than specimens in the open ground. The large clumps of *H.* sieboldiana and *H.* 'Frances Williams' seen at international flower shows will have come from the ground and only been grown short-term in a container, usually no longer than a season before they will be returned to the ground.

RECOMMENDED VARIETIES

Generally hostas that make small crowns and fine roots give no trouble and make the most satisfactory container plants; indeed they often grow better. All the *H.* fortunei types are ideal and even after ten years a *H.* 'Francee' of mine, now growing in a 20-litre pot, is still a superb specimen.

There will always be exceptions but for long-term pot culture I would not recommend hostas that have *H.* sieboldiana in their make-up, e.g. *H.* 'Frances Williams' and *H.* 'Big Mama'. Some of the Tardiana group are also difficult (although *H.* 'Halcyon' can make an excellent pot plant), as are the large-leaved golds such as *H.* 'Midas Touch', *H.* 'Piedmont Gold', *H.* 'Golden Sunburst', and *H.* 'August Moon'. Hostas that make very thick roots are best grown in the ground after four years, as only in the ground will they develop the full potential of their foliage. *H.* sieboldiana forms have been used in the development of many hybrids so a watchful eye would need to be kept on any of that parentage which you grow in containers when young.

H. 'Christmas Tree' with *Carex comans* in the foreground. The white hydrangea, *Cornus alba* 'Elegantissima' and bamboo in the background contribute to an effective group for the white garden.

Pests

SLUGS AND SNAILS

Unfortunately a hosta leaf is caviar to a slug or a snail and measures must be taken to protect the plants from these pests. There are a large number of different species of slugs and snails and some do more damage than others. The small brown and grey slugs are a far greater nuisance than their larger relatives, and of the snails the garden snail and the strawberry snail are the most serious. The latter is much smaller, with a pale brown, flattened shell and hides in the crown of the plant, making it very hard to kill. Nothing looks worse than a plant that is reduced to lace curtains although the odd hole or so does not spoil the garden effectiveness and is nearly impossible to avoid if your garden is a paradise to these pests.

There is only one answer and it may take a season or two of constant warfare before vigilance and preventive measures can be reduced to the odd battle or so. First and foremost it is important to be tidy, to clear away all possible breeding sites – rotting vegetation is the perfect home for a slug or a snail. If mulches are applied around your plants, these pests must be eradicated first or your efforts to get your hostas to grow well will be defeated.

The most effective control is certainly slug pellets, but for those gardeners who do not wish to use them there are other preventive measures. Slug pellets contain either metaldehyde or methiocarb; methiocarb is more toxic than metaldehyde, which breaks down more quickly in the soil. They are usually blue, a colour unattractive to birds, and they also contain animal repellent substances. They are very effective and slugs and snails do not usually recover, but they must be applied frequently. The easiest way to scatter them is to put one flower pot inside another, fill the inner pot with pellets and use the drainage holes in the pots to sprinkle the pellets thinly over the whole garden; animals are less likely to eat them than when in heaps and control is far more effective. They can be placed in shelters created by a stone which protects them from rain and then the dead slugs and snails can be easily removed before animals can eat them.

Pellets must be used on a very regular basis, always after rain, and at intervals no greater than every ten days; they need to be spread very early every season, before the shoots emerge in the spring and applications should continue right through the growing season to reduce the breeding cycle. Gradually there will be fewer adults produced, although some years will always be worse than others. In spells of dry weather damage is usually less because the slugs will stay deep in the soil and snails will withdraw into their shells.

A reasonably effective method which is more acceptable to gardeners with pets is to use a liquid product. There are a number on the market but they must be watered very thoroughly on to the plant and its surroundings and used at frequent intervals. Most are based on aluminium sulphate, which is relatively non-toxic. Other products, such as slug tape and slug gels, exist but although probably effective for protection round a few prized plants, they are not the answer for slug- and snail-infested gardens.

There are non-chemical methods, but unfortunately most will only give some measure of control. A torch light inspection at night will allow physical removal of the offenders as they come out at night to feed but, although effective this is time-consuming in any but the smallest garden. Destroy the slugs and snails collected – throwing them over the hedge only means they will return!

Damage can be limited by surrounding the plants with a rough material that slugs do not like travelling over. Eggshells, coal ashes or gravel are all deterrents, but it is no good whatsoever putting this over occupants in residence.

Natural predators can help also to reduce the problem: birds, hedgehogs, frogs and toads should be encouraged. I have found toads particularly effective and find they do not seem to pick up poisoned slugs and snails; I have a thriving toad population, despite using a considerable number of pellets. Although these natural predators help, they are not usually present in large enough numbers to stop all damage to leaves.

Failing all else, as some gardens seem to have far more slugs and snails than others, it is far easier to protect plants in pots. Even slug pellets can be tucked out of site in the rim of the pot and removed and replaced at frequent intervals; most domestic pets or birds will not investigate inside. Pots stood on gravel or paving with the foliage of each not touching can often escape unscathed without any need for slug and snail control. If damage is spotted lifting up the pot or going out at night will usually reveal the culprits, which can then be removed. When hostas are dormant it is a good idea to tip the plant out of the pot to see if any eggs have been laid and to remove them before they develop and become the next generation of pests.

Some hostas are more resistant to damage than others. Thick, leathery leaves are less attractive to slugs and snails than thin papery ones. *H.* 'Sum and Substance', for example, has a very large, extremely thick leaf that also stands well above the ground when mature, and suffers much less than many other varieties. *H.* 'Celebration', *H. sieboldii* forms and other small, thin-leaved hostas are the most vulnerable. The following are worth considering and although less prone to slug damage than most, some can certainly be damaged by snails, the tiny snails being a very difficult problem.

Hostas least damaged by slugs and snails

'Barbara White'	*hypoleuca*
'Big Daddy'	*kikutii* 'Pruinose'
'Blue Angel'	'Krossa Regal'
'Blue Cadet'	'Love Pat'
'Blue Umbrellas'	'Midas Touch'
'Bold Ruffles'	*nigrescens*
'Christmas Tree'	'Pizzazz'
fluctuans 'Variegated'	*rupifraga*
fortunei 'Aureo-marginata'	'Sea Lotus Leaf'
	sieboldiana (and forms)
'Frances Williams'	'Snow Cap'
'Fringe Benefit'	'Spritzer'
'Gold Edger'	'Sum and Substance'
'Gold Regal'	Tardiana group
'Golden Sculpture'	*tardiflora*
'Green Fountain'	*tokudama* (and forms)
'Green Piecrust'	'Zounds'
'Green Sheen'	

RABBITS, HARES AND DEER

The only way is to fence. Rabbits can reduce a specimen hosta to the ground at a sitting. Every time new leaves are pushed up it will return for another meal until the hosta leaves will eventually get smaller and smaller and disappear. Rabbit fencing must be close-meshed (small ones can get through very small holes), buried below ground and at least 90 cm (3 ft) high. Fencing against deer, also very partial to hosta leaves, needs to be at least 2 m (6½ ft) high. In some respects it is not surprising that hosta leaves are such a favourite food, as they are used in cooking by the Japanese.

MICE AND VOLES

Mice can eat hostas, especially in winter and those that are mulched are usually more vulnerable. It is a Catch

22 situation: mulching can protect against frost, retain moisture and result in better growth but it is also a home for mice, slugs and snails. Voles are not a general problem but if you have them then you will soon become aware that they are fond of hosta roots. A large specimen hosta of mine became a winter repository for at least thirty acorns and all the roots under the crown were eaten. Wire mesh guards will protect the roots.

VINE WEEVILS

These are far more of a problem when growing plants in pots than in the ground. If any larvae – they are white and C-shaped – are discovered they should be killed immediately as they eat roots. The adults can notch the foliage and this can be unsightly.

Plants frequently repotted do not seem to have the same problems as those that are left in the same compost for a number of years. A number of proprietary soil pest killers can be incorporated in the compost and preventive measures taken every few months. Recent research developments will probably result in satisfactory biological controls based on a nematode becoming the solution to the problem. If it is suspected that weevil larvae are in the roots, you must shake off all the compost, destroy the larvae and repot in fresh compost. Hostas are not the favourite food of a vine weevil and it is usually only a problem in neglected plants. Woodlice can also notch the petioles and the leaves but they are not a serious problem.

OTHER PESTS

Hostas are generally trouble-free and although sap-sucking insects can cause visual damage they do not

H. 'Tall Boy' in the RHS garden, Wisley, where the mass planting is very effective when in flower. Good ground cover.

usually harm the plant in the long term. The easiest control is a strong jet of water to wash off the offenders. This is more often a problem under protection than in the garden.

Diseases

Hostas are relatively free of any problems and as long as they are given good culture and kept free from slug and snail damage they are likely to flourish for many years, but occasionally a virus infection will result in leaves with mosaic-like markings, chlorotic spots or a stunted appearance (this can also be caused by crown congestion). It is important to realize that late frosts, leaf scorch and mineral deficiency can show the same symptoms but if a viral infection is suspected the only answer is to destroy the plant. Insects or a propagating knife can transmit the virus to perfectly healthy plants. Some of the Tardiana group seem more prone to virus, as do H. 'Sea Sprite', H. opipara and H. crispula.

Spots on leaves have a number of causes. Leaf spot disease can be treated by spraying with Benomyl or Thiram as it is caused by fungi, but most spots on hosta leaves are caused by frost or sun damage. A slight frost will not destroy the leaf but break down some of the cell structure and the damage will not be obvious immediately. The sun, especially if the leaves are wet, can cause brown burn spots where the individual water droplets have acted like a lens. Insects can cause pinhead spots, as can chemicals, and fumes and oily residues may also damage the leaf surface. Brown edges to leaves are usually the result of frost or wind damage, although seasons that are abnormal, whether spells of extremes temperature and of drought, seem to contribute. There is nothing wrong in removing the odd damaged leaf although it is a mistake to remove all of them.

Crown rot, which can be caused by a fungus, can occur, especially in places with high temperatures. If the leaves turn yellow and the crowns detach from the middle, the plant must be pulled apart, only the healthy pieces retained and each piece treated with a fungicide before being repotted in new pots and fresh compost. Sometimes poorly drained soil or too dense a compost which has been over-watered, can cause the same problem, especially with *H. sieboldii* forms which do not have a very vigorous root system and a tendency to crown congestion. At Chelsea Flower Show in 1989, when the temperature in the marquee exceeded 38°C (100°F), some of the hostas developed the early signs of crown rot; they were packed with moss around the crowns to hide the pots and this inhibited air circulating around the plants; a gap is now left around the stems to prevent this happening.

Having described some of the possible threats to hostas, it is worth reiterating that, other than damage caused by slugs and snails and late frosts, most gardeners will never meet any other problems. Compared with many garden plants, most hostas are easy, problem-free perennials that grow surprisingly well in a number of situations.

Propagation

DIVISION

Spring, when the crowns are just beginning to emerge, is the ideal time to split. If the clump is mature the easiest way is to take a sharp spade and slice a piece off, leaving the rest in the ground. This piece can then be cut up further or pulled apart into individual crowns. Some hostas pull apart easily; others need a sharp kitchen knife. The plant left in the ground will quickly recover; by the end of the season you will not notice the missing piece, and the clump will maintain its mature leaf form. The rest will give you pieces to grow on but they will take a few years to return to adult leaf form and must be treated like newly acquired plants. If only a few plants are needed then the slice taken off can be replanted as it is and this will not go back to a juvenile leaf form but any woody root must be cut away and the plant treated in the same way as those being divided from containers.

Some hostas are very slow to make divisions and a number of other methods have been tried, mainly by nurserymen, to induce the plant to make propagating material. The Ross Method was originally developed in USA and the details published in the *American Hosta Journal*. It is easier to carry out this technique on a thick, single crown hosta growing in a pot although it can be used quite satisfactorily on plants in the ground. I have found the best time is in spring or early summer when the plant is in active growth. The soil or compost is scraped back to reveal the basal plate of the stem; the roots are below this. A thin, sharp straight knive is inserted into the stem just above the basal plate and the knife pushed down through the plate into the roots (Fig. 11). Another cut can then be made at right angles to the first. Where the stem has been damaged the tissue will mend by callousing, a scar will form and this encourages a growth bud which in turn will become a new division. The hosta should be tended carefully and although slight yellowing of the leaves often occurs, the plant continues to grow.

A slight adaption of this method is to push the knife in as far as the middle of the crown only and to slice down, repeating the process round the stem. A very thick stem can have six to eight slits, but two or three would be plenty for a less developed plant. Instead of one large crown the plant should develop a number of smaller plants, according to the knife cuts. The resulting new crowns need to be grown on usually for at least one season before they are split up, to give them time to develop their own root systems.

OTHER METHODS

Hostas can be grown from seed but generally they will not come true. Most people who have bought packets of seed or collected their own are very disappointed with the resulting progeny. Many new hostas are being raised by deliberate or accidental crossings but for every new hosta raised many thousands of seedlings are culled. The proportion of variegated seedlings arising, for example, from *H.* 'Frances Williams', is infinitessimal, most plants turning out to be blues, greens and a tiny percentage of golds. It is better not to pass on seedlings by name until they have been registered and this should only be for plants that are worthy.

The most common method of propagation of the newer hostas today is micropropagation. Without the advent of tissue culture, the newer hostas would not have become as popular as they have. Many thousands can be propagated in a matter of months and a nucleus stock built up by the nurseryman. These young plants need special care in their early days and most should not be planted out in the garden until they have had two seasons of growth. They have been propagated in sterile conditions and need a period of adaption to the outside world.

Many hostas are inately unstable, they sport readily and in the tissue culture laboratory this is magnified, with the result that the very technique of propagating is giving rise to many more new varieties. If proved worthy these are in turn propagated. Three very fine hostas which will be in great demand in years to come that have arisen in this way are a cream-edged *H.* 'Honeybells' called *H.* 'Sugar and Cream', a cream-edged *H.* 'Krossa Regal' (*H.* 'Regal Splendor') and a gold-centred *H.* 'Halcyon' (*H.* 'June').

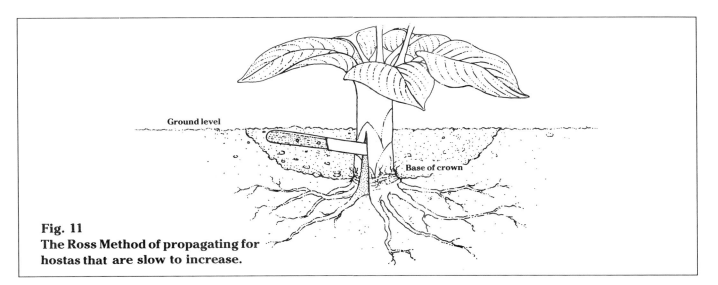

Ground level

Base of crown

**Fig. 11
The Ross Method of propagating for hostas that are slow to increase.**

CHAPTER 6

List of Hostas

This is by no means a comprehensive list of the hostas available as there are now over 1100 registered names, but it is a selection of those that are readily obtainable and of those that are in specialist nurseries and likely to be popular in the future. I have included some of the old favourites, species that I feel should be more widely grown, and some of the newer cultivars that have a future in the garden or for the flower arranger. Present breeding aims are for increased pest resistance and sun tolerance, fragrance in the flowers, new colour breaks such as blue and white variegation and an ever-increasing range of small hostas which should appeal to the alpine gardener and those with tiny plots. I have listed a selection of the many kinds and although some are expensive, the advent of propagation by tissue culture means they will not be expensive tomorrow and some will become as common in gardens of the future as *H.* 'Frances Williams' is today.

Not all are easy to grow but if they are distinctive and desired by certain gardeners who are prepared to take care then I feel they have a part to play. An example is *H.* 'Reversed', loved by flower arrangers who know it, and if grown in a pot in dappled shade it can look spectacular, but it is certainly not a good landscape plant.

Most hostas in cultivation are not species, although the name may suggest otherwise. I have left those that have historic associations with their well-known name even if we now know they are not species, but for more recent cultivars I have followed the practice of the international registration body for hostas in USA. As we learn more about hostas it is inevitable that nomenclature changes will be made. The gardener often finds this confusing but in the long term taxonomic accuracy will help to resolve the problems.

Many hostas have suffered from errors of nomenclature since their introduction. The species are chiefly natives of Japan but some come from China and Korea and partly because of their variability in the wild they have been wrongly identified. Mature plants often look very different from the juvenile form and this again causes confusion, and plants are frequently sold under erroneous names. Some older hybrids have also been described as species but with the present enormous interest in the genus a start has been made in trying to solve some of the many points of confusion.

There is much argument at the moment over identification within the Tardiana group raised by Eric Smith, and it is quite possible that in the future changes must be made. The original cross was of *H. tardiflora* and *H. sieboldiana* 'Elegans' and the resulting progeny were given a TF number, the first generation being designated TF 1×, the second TF 2× and the third, of which only one seems to exist, TF 3×1. Some of the progeny of the second generation also indicate that a *H. nakaiana* form could have become involved in the cross: e.g. *H.* 'Blue Belle' (TF 2×22) and *H.* 'Eric Smith' (TF 2×31). The problem of identification in this group is complex. Many of the plants are very similar to each other, and were distributed under number when very young, the names being given later, some in Europe and some in USA, with the result that we now have either more than one plant with the same name or the same plant with two or more names. I believe we may discover that *H.* 'Blue Moon' and *H.* 'Dorset Blue' have been mixed up in the trade as they are very similar;

H. 'Dorset Blue' is the more vigorous. H. Blue Dimples' and H. 'Blue Wedgwood' are certainly muddled up, something that is very easy to understand when their relevant numbers were TF 2×8 and TF 2×9 and they look very like each other in the immature state. I have only listed a selection of superior hybrids in the group, of which, H. 'Halcyon' is the best known and most widely planted.

The following list of hostas includes a brief description of each and where applicable special cultural requirements. Parentage has sometimes been included as this can be a useful guide to a hosta's appearance and its growing characteristics. The dimensions given denote height×spread (H/S) of the

H. 'Spritzer' (a young plant) with *Hakonechloa macra* 'Alboaurea', *Carex testacea* and ferns edging a path, seen against a backdrop of *Cornus alba* 'Aurea' and *Elaeagnus ebbingei*.

mature foliage mound, this being the dominant element in the garden although it will vary in different climatic regions. The spread indicates the required planting distances. Those marked * are especially suitable for flower arranging.

H. 'Allan P. McConnell'
H/S 13×20 cm (5×8 in)
Attractive small green leaves with a narrow white margin. 20 cm (8 in) purple scapes with lavender

59

flowers in midsummer. Useful for edging or on a shady rock garden.

H. 'Amanuma'
H/S 15 × 30 cm (6 × 12 in)
A *H. nakaiana* seedling. A small green mound with slightly wavy leaves; lavender flowers from early summer onwards on 38 cm (15 in) purple-dotted scapes.

H. 'Antioch'
H/S 50 × 90 cm (20 × 36 in)
Form of *H. fortunei* 'Albo-marginata'. Medium to large cascading mound of cream-edged green heart-shaped leaves. Lavender flowers in midsummer. Similar to *H.* 'Spinners' which is larger, *H.* 'Moorheim' ('Moorheimii') and to *H.* 'Goldbrook' which is smaller and has a wider gold edge turning cream. Looks wonderful in partial shade planted with ferns and *Geranium phaeum album* where it lightens a dark corner.

H. 'August Moon'
H/S 65 × 90 cm (26 × 36 in)
Young foliage is pale green which deepens to gold if grown in dappled shade and develops large corrugated golden leaves when mature. 90 cm (3 ft) pale lavender, trumpet-shaped flowers in mid-summer. Vigorous and fast-growing. Will grow in sun in cooler climates. A number of sports have arisen, and some will have a future in the garden: *H.* 'Abiqua Moonbeam' ('Mayan Moon') is blue-green with lime green margins; *H.* 'Lunar Eclipse' has a white edge to the gold leaf; *H.* 'September Sun' is a gold with a dark green edge, a very attractive new variety.

H. 'Barbara White'
H/S 50 × 75 cm (20 × 30 in)
Seedling arose at Goldbrook Plants nursery, UK and was named in honour of Barbara White, a secretary of the Hardy Plant Society for many years. The chartreuse gold, heavily textured, orbicular leaves appeal to flower arrangers. Near-white flowers. Although slow to mature eventually becomes an impressive plant. Needs dappled light to colour.

H. 'Bennie MacRae'
H/S 60 × 75 cm (24 × 30 in)
Seedling of open-pollinated *H. plantaginea*. Lance-shaped glossy, wavy, green leaves. Fragrant lavender flowers on very tall scapes from late summer onwards. Has larger leaves than *H.* 'Honeybells' and darker coloured flowers that are sweetly scented.

H. 'Big Daddy' *
H/S 75 × 90 cm (30 × 36 in)
Large round, puckered blue leaves that are pest-resistant. Pale lavender flowers 90 cm (3 ft) high appear in early summer. Best sited in shade but not under the drip of trees. Makes a good architectural specimen against walls, underplanted with *Pulmonaria* 'Lewis Palmer'.

H. 'Big Mama'
H/S 90 × 100 cm (36 × 40 in)
Form of *H. sieboldiana*. Large blue-green, cupped and pointed leaves of heavy substance, with pale lavender flowers in early summer. Good background plant to other hostas, dicentras and ferns in the shade garden.

H. 'Bill Brincka'
H/S 70 × 150 cm (28 × 60 in)
Selection of *H. opipara*. Large, bright green leaves edged with a wide margin of gold that becomes creamier as the season progresses. Scapes 75 cm (30 in) tall carry racemes of bell-shaped, light lavender flowers with darker stripes in midsummer. This form has been given a separate name as, unlike some forms, it has no virus. Looks wonderful as an accent in a green border of ferns. Very distinctive when mature.

H. 'Black Hills'
H/S 75 × 125 cm (30 × 50 in)
Deep green, puckered, heavy textured leaves. Lilac flowers in midsummer on scapes just above the foliage mound. One of the darkest green hostas available, but not well known.

H. 'Blond Elf'
H/S 20 × 60 cm (8 × 24 in)
Small gold, wavy-edged lanceolate leaves make a wide-spreading low mound. Lavender flowers in midsummer. Best in dappled light as an edger or in an alpine bed.

H. 'Blue Angel'*
H/S 1 × 1.2 m (40 × 48 in)
Form of *H. sieboldiana*. Very large, glaucous bluish leaves make this a very impressive landscape hosta and it is certainly worth waiting for this to grow to maturity. Tall, dense clusters of lilac-white flowers are long lasting. Underplant with *H.* 'Wide Brim' for a dramatic focal point or with *Tiarella cordifolia* for a more subtle woodland scheme. Best in shade. Once established is surprisingly tolerant of a dry situation and because the leaves are not puckered but point downwards they do not collect debris from trees.

H. 'Blue Belle'
H/S 25 × 50 cm (10 × 20 in)
Tardiana group TF 2 × 22. Bluish leaves, attractive mauve-lilac flowers well above the foliage mound. Very similar to *H.* 'Blue Cadet'. Good edging plant in shade.

H. 'Blue Blush'
H/S 20 × 45 cm (8 × 18 in)
Tardiana group TF 3 × 1. Excellent blue foliage, mainly lanceolate leaves with lilac flowers just above the foliage mound in midsummer. Slow to establish but an excellent smaller growing hosta suitable for edging in shade. Considered by some to be the bluest of this group. Grow with *Dicentra formosa* 'Stuart Boothman' and *Lamium maculatum* 'Beacon's Silver'.

H. 'Blue Boy'
H/S 30 × 50 cm (12 × 20 in)
Probably a *H. nakaiana* seedling. Small, wavy, glaucous blue-green leaves and pale lavender flowers. Lovely with dicentras or underneath *Cornus alba* 'Aurea' in association with *Molinia caerulea* 'Variegata'.

H. 'Blue Cadet'
H/S 38 × 55 cm (15 × 22 in)
Blue-green, heart-shaped leaves form a dense rounded mound. Dark lavender flowers in midsummer. Excellent edger in dappled shade.

H. 'Blue Danube'
H/S 25 × 50 cm (10 × 20 in)
Tardiana group TF 2 × 24. Very blue, slightly rounded leaves with pale lavender flowers with a darker but still pale stripe, slightly above the foliage mound in early summer. One of the first of this group to flower. A very pretty plant for edging a shady walk or in association with *Carex comans*.

H. 'Blue Dimples'
H/S 30 × 60 cm (12 × 24 in)
Tardiana group TF 2 × 8. Thick blue leaves of heavy substance with dimples on mature plants. Pale lavender flowers in midsummer. Partial to deep shade.

H. 'Blue Moon'*
H/S 10 × 30 cm (4 × 12 in)
Tardiana group TF 2 × 2. Small neat, rounded but flattish grey-blue leaves. Dense clusters of bluish-mauve flowers appear in midsummer just above the foliage mound. Slow. The foliage colour is intensified

Three very new hostas for accents among the blues. Left to right at the front: 'Goldbrook Glimmer', 'Snow Cap' and 'Pizzazz' with *Pulmonaria mollis* 'Royal Blue' and ferns.

in shade. Not vigorous and probably rare as most plants in commerce are probably in fact *H.* 'Dorset Blue' which is very similar but a much stronger-growing variety.

H. 'Blue Skies'
H/S 20 × 40 cm (8 × 16 in)
Tardiana group TF 2 × 6. Roundish, pointed, blue leaves which grow fairly flat to the ground. Hyacinth-like pale lavender flowers in late summer. Best in shade. Has given rise to an all-green sport, *H.* 'Emerald Skies', with shiny emerald green foliage which is very slow.

H. 'Blue Umbrellas'
H/S 90 × 100 cm (36 × 40 in)
Form of *H. sieboldiana.* Very large, bold blue-green leaves of heavy substance. Pale lavender flowers above the foliage mound in early summer. Although this will tolerate sun, it is far more impressive in dappled shade as a background plant to *Dicentra spectabilis* and *H.* 'Pearl Lake'.

H. 'Blue Wedgwood' *
H/S 25×55 cm (10×22 in)
Tardiana group TF 2×9. Lovely wedge-shaped, heavily seersuckered blue leaves. Takes a number of years to develop adult foliage. Often muddled with *H.* 'Blue Dimples' when juvenile. Lavender flowers in midsummer. Good planted with pale pink astilbes.

H. 'Bold Ribbons'
H/S 25×60 cm (10×24 in)
Green lance-shaped leaves with a creamy yellow edge that fades to creamy white. Tall violet flowers in midsummer. Makes good ground cover as is stoloniferous. Needs plain neighbours as the foliage is striking. Very similar are *H.* 'Neat Splash Rim' and *H.* 'Yellow Splash Rim', the stable forms of *H.* 'Neat Splash' and *H.* 'Yellow Splash'. All are popular with flower arrangers and easy to grow.

H. 'Bold Ruffles' *
H/S 60×90 cm (24×36 in)
Large blue-grey ruffled leaves. Pale lavender flowers in midsummer. Needs to be grown in good soil in part or full shade. Not good as a container plant but suitable for flower arrangers.

H. 'Bright Glow'
H/S 38×55 cm (15×22 in)
Tardiana type. Thick, textured, heart-shaped leaves change to gold. White flowers in early summer. Needs some sun to colour but not hot and dry. Slow.

H. 'Bright Lights'
H/S 30×50 cm (12×20 in)
Bright gold-centred leaves with blue-green margins. Probably from *H. tokudama* 'Flavo-circinalis' but with reversed colouring. Light lavender flowers in midsummer. Slow. Best in the dappled light and makes a striking mound. One for the flower arrangers. Use as the highlight plant among blue hostas and gold sedges.

H. 'Brim Cup' *
H/S 30×38 cm (12×15 in)
The slightly cupped and puckered green leaves have a wide creamy yellow margin that fades to white. Lavender flowers on 45 cm (18 in) scapes in midsummer. This will become popular. Best in shade or dappled light and looks delightful with *Athyrium filix-femina* 'Minutissimum' and small white astilbes.

H. 'Buckshaw Blue'
H/S 35×60 cm (14×24 in)
Probably a *H. tokudama* seedling. Very blue cupped foliage of heavy substance. Greyish white flowers 45 cm (18 in) high appear in summer. Slow to mature and best in shade. Looks good with pink or blue hardy geraniums.

H. 'Candy Hearts'
H/S 38×55 cm (15×22 in)
Seedling of *H. nakaiana*. Heart-shaped green leaves, 45 cm (18 cm) bell-shaped lavender flowers in midsummer. Two recent sports of this are *H.* 'Amber Maiden', which has a chartreuse edge deepening to yellow during the season, and *H.* 'Heartsong' with a white edge and probably smaller growing.

H. 'Carrie Ann'
H/S 8×20 cm (3×8 in)
Small wavy green leaves have a creamy white margin. Delightful white flowers on 50 cm (20 in) scapes in late summer. Suitable for the shady rock garden with *Mitella caulescens* and tiny ferns.

H. 'Celebration'
H/S 25×45 cm (10×18 in)
Small cream-centred, green lanceolate leaves. Lavender flowers in summer. Striking red seed pods. Must have part shade and needs care as slugs love it. Best grown in a pot as it is not a good garden plant, but the leaves are much loved by flower arrangers.

H. 'Chartreuse Wiggles'
H/S 8×25 cm (3×10 in)
Narrow, ruffled, lance-shaped leaves of chartreuse yellow. Lavender flowers in late summer. This is an interesting little hosta that needs care in early years and is probably best grown on a raised bed in dappled shade. Stoloniferous.

H. 'Chinese Sunrise'
H/S 38×70 cm (15×28 in)
Form of *H. lancifolia*. Narrow, lance-shaped, glossy chartreuse gold leaves with a green margin. Colour fades to all green in the summer. Stoloniferous and vigorous. Abundant dark lavender flowers in late summer. Associates well with *Hakonechloa macra* 'Alboaurea', *H.* 'Inaho' and dark green filigree ferns.

H. 'Christmas Tree' *
H/S 45×90 cm (18×36 in)
A *H.* 'Frances Williams' cross. Large, heavily corrugated green leaves with a creamy white edge. Light lavender flowers from midsummer onwards with very leafy scapes that give the impression of a Christmas tree. Looks super all season and even the flower stems decorated with black seed pods should appeal to the flower arranger. For a dramatic group grow with *Veratrum nigrum*, *Salix elaeagnos angustifolia*, ferns and *Ophiopogon planiscapus nigrescens* in light shade.

H. clausa normalis
H/S 20×60 cm (8×24 in)
Shiny dark green leaves with striking purple funnel-shaped flowers on 60 cm (24 in) scapes in midsummer. Useful ground cover as it is stoloniferous and the flowers are very attractive. Like nearly all green hostas a very underrated plant.

H. 'Colossal'
H/S 90×100 cm (36×40 in)
An enormous mound of large green leaves with pale lavender flowers in midsummer. Plain green hostas are very useful as green mounds are restful. Underplant with *Pachysandra terminalis* 'Variegata' for complete ground cover.

H. crispula
H/S 60×90 cm (24×36 in)
Large heart-shaped, dark green, wavy leaves with an irregular white margin. Tall trumpet-shaped pale mauve flowers in midsummer. Spectacular when well-grown but needs careful siting in dappled shade, out of the winds and danger from early frosts. Looks lovely with Solomon's seal and blue flowers.

H. 'Daybreak'
H/S 50×75 cm (20×30 in)
Dense clump of shiny deep gold foliage. Leaves are of a good texture. Lavender blue flowers on 70 cm (28 in) scapes. Not well known but highly thought of in USA. Vigorous. Best in dappled light for leaf colour. For a striking group underplant with a lily-of-the-valley such as *Convallaria majalis* 'Lineata'.

H. decorata
H/S 30×75 cm (12×30 in)
Medium-sized broadly oval green leaf with a white margin. The blunt rounded end distinguishes this from *H. undulata* 'Albo-marginata' ('Thomas Hogg') with which it is confused. Scapes 60 cm (24 in) tall with narrow bell-shaped, dark violet flowers in midsummer. Rarely planted today as usually not very vigorous but if happy in cool woodland soil it will make wide spreading mats as it is stoloniferous. *H.* 'Betsy King' is an all-green seedling with a very free-flowering habit.

H. 'Dorset Blue'
H/S 20×45 cm (8×18 in)
Tardiana group TF 2×4. Small, very blue, slightly

cupped leaves with greyish lavender flowers in midsummer just above the foliage mound. One of the best of the smaller blues. Lovely in dappled shade as an edger or in an alpine bed with small geraniums such as *Geranium renardii*.

H. 'Duchess'

H/S 13×25 cm (5×10 in)
Sport of *H. nakaiana* seedling. Small mound of dark green, lanceolate leaves edged creamy white. Scapes 45 cm (18 in) tall with medium purple flowers in midsummer. Suitable for tiny gardens and alpine beds. Dappled shade.

H. 'Elfin Power'

H/S 20×38 cm (8×15 in)
Narrow lanceolate mid-green leaves with a white margin. Racemes of lavender flowers 60 cm (24 in) tall in late summer. Very pretty. *H.* 'Pixie Power' has a small green leaf with a white middle and only grows 10 cm (4 in) high. Both are slow and need some shade.

H. 'Emily Dickinson'

H/S 50×75 cm (20×30 in)
Medium green leaf with irregular cream margin. Many fragrant bright lavender flowers on 70 cm (28 in) stems in midsummer. Will become popular when it ceases to be so expensive.

H. fluctuans 'Variegated' *

H/S 90×100 cm (36×40 in)
Large upright, vase-shaped mound of green centred, heavy-textured leaves edged in creamy gold and topped by 1.5 m (5 ft) of pale lavender flowers in midsummer. This is slow to mature but when it does is spectacular. A very choice, as yet expensive, variety that should be in every garden. It makes a striking focal point among ferns and is better used as a specimen plant with contrasting foliage in a shady spot. The Japanese use it as a container plant.

H. fortunei

H/S 60×90 cm (24×36 in)
A group of hostas that are not species but for convenience retain their name. Good foliage plants with heart-shaped leaves that make medium-large mounds with generally mauve-violet flowers well above the foliage in late summer. Emerge late so are rarely damaged by frosts. Make good container plants. Name now usually applied to a plain green-leaved plant although not technically correct.

H. fortunei 'Albo-marginata' ('Marginato-albo')

H/S 55×80 cm (22×32 in)
Darkish green leaves with a white back are edged with an irregular white margin that is variable in the same plant and from season to season. When at its best is superb but often disappoints. Must have moist shade.

H. fortunei 'Albo-picta'

H/S 55×90 cm (22×36 in)
In spring the leaves are creamy yellow with a green margin but they fade to dull green as the season advances. This is accelerated in very warm weather. Trumpet-shaped pale mauve flowers in midsummer. *H.* 'Chelsea Babe' looks like a smaller version, so named because it is at its best in late May in Britain, at the time of the Chelsea Flower Show. Probably of mixed parentage and not very vigorous. *H.* 'Phyllis Campbell' looks like a more vigorous *H. fortunei* 'Albo-picta', with leaves of thicker texture that fade later. All need partial shade.

H. fortunei 'Aurea'

H/S 40×75 cm (16×30 in)
Medium-sized soft yellow leaves that fade to green. Pale purple flowers 60 cm (24 in) high in midsummer. Very attractive used as underplanting for shrubs and especially useful where a gold theme is required in early summer but not later. Two improved forms of

Young plants of *H.* 'Regal Splendor' (cream edge) and *H.* 'Hadspen Blue' with *Astilbe simplicifolia* 'Sprite', *Acer negundo* 'Flamingo' and *Rubus thibetanus* 'Silver Fern'.

this are *H.* 'Gold Haze' and *H.* 'Gold Leaf'. The first is much larger and more vigorous than the type and forms a cascading mound which is very impressive in the early garden. *H.* 'Gold Leaf' has a sheen to the leaf. Both fade to green later in the season.

H. fortunei 'Aureo-marginata'*
H/S 55×90 cm (22×36 in)
Light yellow edge to mid-green leaf. Violet trumpet-shaped flowers rise to 90 cm (3 ft) in midsummer. Makes an excellent, vigorous mound especially effective planted with *Ligularia przewalskii* 'The Rocket', *Iris pseudacorus* 'Variegata' and *Matteuccia struthiopteris* (ostrich feather fern) in a moist border where it will take a fair amount of sun. Excellent for flower arrangers and it also makes a good container plant.

H. fortunei 'Hyacinthina'
H/S 60×90 cm (24×36 in)
Slightly rugose grey-green leaves with fine white line on the edge. Good funnel-shaped violet flowers well above the foliage mound in midsummer. An invalu-

able plant for mass planting and as a foil to hotter colours. *H. fortunei* 'Hyacinthina Variegata' has a wider creamy margin to the leaf that fades as the season advances.

H. 'Fragrant Bouquet'
H/S 45×65 cm (18×26 in)
Dense mound of apple green leaves edged creamy yellow, with very large, fragrant whitish flowers in summer on 90 cm (3 ft) scapes. This is still very expensive but will become popular as the flowers are superb. It is reputed to be sun-tolerant and pest-resistant. Lovely with ferns and green and yellow variegated grasses and for picking.

H. **'Mildred Seaver', a relatively new variety, planted with *Polystichum braunii*, a dark green glossy fern that emphasizes the wide creamy band of the hosta leaf.**

H. 'Fragrant Gold'
H/S 48×65 cm (17×26 in)
Seedling of *H.* 'Sum and Substance'. Medium-sized, heavily textured leaves in chartreuse gold that tolerate sun. 75 cm (30 in) tall fragrant bluish trumpet-shaped flowers with very leafy scapes which appear in late summer.

67

H. 'Francee' *
H/S 55 × 90 cm (22 × 36 in)
A *H. fortunei* form. Excellent white-edged heart-shaped leaves of a rich green. Pale lavender flowers on 75 cm (30 in) scapes. One of the best in the garden and in a container. Associates beautifully with *Aruncus aethusifolius, Geranium sanguineum album,* ferns and taller astilbes, and can make an impressive feature in a group of white and green plants. Invaluable. Emerges late with very attractive young shoots and is rarely damaged by late frosts. Rapid grower. Other similar hostas are *H.* 'North Hills' and *H.* 'Carol' both with white edges.

H. 'Frances Williams' *
H/S 75 × 100 cm (30 × 40 in)
Superb sport of *H. sieboldiana* 'Elegans'. Round, puckered, heavily textured blue-green leaves with a wide margin of muted yellow. Near-white flowers from early summer. Underplant with smaller blue hostas such as *H.* 'Halcyon' and *H.* 'Blue Wedgwood', or with *Dicentra formosa* 'Langtrees'. If grown in too much sun the leaf margin scorches but if given a moist spot and dappled shade can become one of the most impressive hostas. *H.* 'Samurai' is very similar but is faster growing and stands more sun. Some forms appear better than others but it could be in time that all will grow as well; divisions from older clumps appear superior to those from more juvenile plants or from tissue culture.

H. 'Fresh'
H/S 20 × 50 cm (8 × 20 in)
Gold, undulating, lance-shaped leaves with a creamy white rim. Lavender flowers in midsummer. Needs shade to dappled light and makes an interesting edging plant or could be used in a rock garden as an effective contrast to mossy saxifrages and other alpines.

H. 'Fringe Benefit'
H/S 60 × 90 cm (24 × 36 in)
Good, textured heart-shaped green leaves, medium to large with a wide creamy white edge. Lavender flowers in early summer. A good increaser that appears more resistant to slugs than some and useful for planting large areas. Will grow in fairly sunny spots but the foliage is certainly more attractive in some shade. An easy, adaptable hosta that can be used in many ways. Grow with *Arum italicum* 'Pictum' and *Polygonatum × hybridum.*

H. 'Frosted Jade'
H/S 80 × 100 cm (32 × 40 in)
Very large mound of frosted grey-green leaves with a white edge. Pale lavender flowers in midsummer. Grow in dappled shade with *Cornus alba* 'Elegantissima' and *Brunnera macrophylla.*

H. 'Geisha'
H/S 35 × 45 cm (14 × 18 in)
Yellow-green, glossy leaves margined with darker green that are slightly ruffled and with a good texture. Twisted, upright habit makes this a very distinctive hosta. Light purple flowers from midsummer onwards. A desirable plant with a future. Group with other green-gold hostas such as *H.* 'Spritzer', *H.* 'Inaho' and *H.* 'Chinese Sunrise', ferns and yellow grasses.

H. 'George Smith'
H/S 90 × 100 cm (36 × 40 in)
The first of the *H. sieboldiana* 'Elegans' sports with a gold centre and blue margin to be registered. It arose in the garden of George Smith, the well-known flower arranger, and should become available in the future. Superb foliage at its best in dappled shade. White flowers in early summer just above the foliage. *H.* 'Borwick Beauty' and *H.* 'Color Glory' are similar, if not in fact the same, and only time will tell if they

should all be called *H.* 'George Smith'. Invaluable for the flower arranger. Use as specimen hosta with plainer neighbours.

H. 'Ginko Craig'*

H/S 25 × 45 cm (10 × 18 cm)

Lance-shaped, white-edged leaves with attractive tall purple flowers in late summer. Fast grower, useful as an edging plant and to underplant larger white-edged hostas in a border with some shade. Grows well in a pot.

H. 'Gloriosa'

H/S 45 × 60 cm (18 × 24 in)

Form of *H. fortunei*. Thin white edge to cupped, dark green leaf. Mauve flowers in midsummer. This is not easy to grow well but when it does is very distinctive and refined. Avoid tree drip but needs some shade and good cultivation.

H. 'Goldbrook'*

H/S 55 × 100 cm (22 × 40 in)

Form of *H. fortunei*. Dense, cascading mound of green leaves with a broad creamy yellow edge that can extend into the leaf giving a marbled effect. Edge fades to creamy white. Pale lavender flowers on 70 cm (28 in) scapes in midsummer. Makes a very impressive container plant and an excellent leaf for the flower arranger. Associate with *Pachysandra terminalis* 'Green Carpet' and *Anemone × hybrida* 'Alba'. *H.* 'Spinners' is similar but larger and emerges later in the spring.

H. 'Goldbrook Gold'

H/S 60 × 75 cm (24 × 30 in)

Seedling of open-pollinated *H. sieboldiana*. Heavily textured heart-shaped gold leaves with a white back. Will stand some sun and although slow is worth waiting for. Far superior to *H.* 'Golden Sunburst' that scorches badly if not grown in shade.

H. 'Goldbrook Grace'

H/S 15 × 25 cm (6 × 10 in)

Sport of *H.* 'Golden Prayers' with an irregular green rim to gold leaf that fades to a beige-green with a creamier centre as the season advances. Pale lavender flowers that just top the mound appear through the summer. Appears vigorous and associates well with *H.* 'Zounds' in a dappled shady position. Also suitable for a rock garden.

H. 'Gold Edger'

H/S 30 × 45 cm (12 × 18 in)

Small heart-shaped, chartreuse gold leaves. Many pale lavender flowers in midsummer. A rapid grower that needs some sun to colour. Useful edging hosta. *H.* 'Birchwood Parky's Gold' is similar but less sun-tolerant (although it will not colour in deep shade), with a thinner leaf texture. Sometimes called *H.* 'Golden Nakaiana' which is not a valid name. Both are vigorous, attractive hostas for ground cover.

H. 'Gold Regal'

H/S 60 × 90 cm (24 × 36 in)

Medium to large chartreuse gold leaves of upright habit. Tall scapes with good bell-shaped lavender flowers in midsummer. When young a rather ungainly plant but makes a good garden plant with leaves that are thick enough that they are not often damaged and will stand some sun as long as conditions are moist. Will not colour in shade. Needs to be underplanted and not used as a specimen or as a container plant.

H. 'Gold Standard'*

H/S 65 × 100 cm (26 × 40 in)

Sport of *H. fortunei*. The heart-shaped leaves emerge green but gradually change to gold edged with green. Pale lavender flowers in midsummer. If well grown and sited this is one of the best of the more recent hostas. It needs dappled light; too much sun and it

H. 'Krossa Regal' growing with *H. montana* 'Aureo-marginata' in Longwood Gardens, USA. Excellent hostas for pots and for flower arrangers.

H. 'Shade Fanfare' a reliable cultivar, photographed in David
Foreman's garden, UK.

whitens, not enough and the gold does not develop. Superb in the garden and container, a flower arrangers' delight. Use as the highlight plant in a green and gold grouping. *H.* 'Richland Gold' is an all-gold sport, similar in habit but the foliage is pale yellow-green. One for dappled shade.

H. 'Golden Bullion' *
H/S 30 × 45 cm (12 × 18 cm)
All-gold sport of *H. tokudama* 'Flavo-circinalis'. Chartreuse yellow cupped leaves, slightly pointed. Pale lavender flowers just above the foliage mound. As yet fairly new but highly rated in USA. Appears to grow better than *H.* 'Golden Medallion'.

H. 'Golden Medallion'
H/S 38 × 60 cm (15 × 24 in)
All-gold sport of *H. todudama* 'Aureo-nebulosa' and *H. tokudama*. Heavily seersuckered, cupped gold leaves with racemes of near-white flowers in early summer. Pest-resistant but very slow. Does not grow well in a container. Many of the plants sold under this name are *H.* 'Golden Sunburst', a much larger and faster-growing hosta.

H. 'Golden Prayers' *
H/S 35 × 60 cm (14 × 24 in)
Small to medium golden leaves which are slightly puckered when mature. Pale lavender flowers in early summer and often repeat blooms. Best in partial shade as it colours well, but if no sunlight will fade to chartreuse. Looks effective in groups underplanting other hostas of a similar colour scheme. A good pot plant and popular with flower arrangers for smaller arrangements. *H.* 'Little Aurora' is very similar but slightly smaller.

H. 'Golden Sculpture' *
H/S 75 × 100 cm (30 × 40 in)
Broad, chartreuse gold leaves, of a good substance that are tolerant of some sun as long as not hot and dry. Makes a large, very impressive mound. Pest-resistant. Near-white trumpet-shaped flowers on 90 cm (3 ft) stems. Use as a focal point underplanted with smaller gold hostas, low-growing white astilbes, yellow day lilies and ferns. Excellent garden and flower arranging plant.

H. 'Golden Sunburst'
H/S 75 × 100 cm (30 × 40 in)
The all-gold sports of *H.* 'Frances Williams', whether occurring naturally or in tissue culture. Large gold leaves that burn in sun and must have dappled light; in full shade tends to fade to green. Whitish flowers in early summer.

H. 'Golden Tiara' *
H/S 30 × 50 cm (12 × 20 in)
Sport of *H. nakaiana*. Compact, heart-shaped green leaves edged gold with 60 cm (24 in) purple flowers in midsummer. Vigorous, attractive smaller hosta very suitable for the front of the border underplanted with *Chrysogonum virginianum*. Has given rise to a number of sports, some naturally and some in tissue culture which now form the Tiara Series. The following are of interest and some have great potential for the garden or a container. *H.* 'Diamond Tiara' has a green leaf with a creamy margin. *H.* 'Emerald Tiara' is the reverse colour pattern of *H.* 'Golden Tiara' with a gold centre and green rim. Appears vigorous. *H.* 'Golden Scepter' is the all-gold version which needs some shade, very bright early in the season but has a rather thin leaf. *H.* 'Jade Scepter' is chartreuse green, vigorous, and it should appeal to flower arrangers. Grow under *Polygonatum falcatum* 'Variegatum'. *H.* 'Platinum Tiara' has a gold leaf with a white margin. Although slow initially this makes an impressive small plant but needs some care and dappled shade. Highly thought of in USA.

H. 'Goldsmith'
H/S 50 × 75 cm (20 × 30 in)
One of Eric Smith's gold hostas with *H. fortunei* 'Aurea' in its parentage. Early gold foliage that holds most of the season topped by leafy scapes with lavender flowers in midsummer. Upright habit and excellent grower. This was originally given to Jerry Webb labelled 'Goldsmith', but was then thought to be *H.* 'Granary Gold', but as a published description of another similar plant with this name exists, the laws of nomenclature mean that the original name stands. Has probably been distributed as *H.* 'Golden Age' and *H.* 'Gold Haze', which fades to green far earlier in the season. *H.* 'Granary Gold' is one of Eric Smith's best gold hostas, with large gold leaves that fade to creamy green towards the end of summer.

H. 'Great Expectations' *
H/S 55 × 85 cm (22 × 34 in)
Sport of *H. sieboldiana* 'Elegans' that arose in the garden of John Bond, the keeper of the Savill Gardens in England, and although it is the same sport as *H.* 'George Smith' it appears different. Green-blue leaves with a gold centre. White blooms from early summer on 82 cm (33 in) scapes. Destined to be the hosta of the nineties. Even a young plant looks distinctive. Plant with *H.* 'Halcyon' and golden grasses.

H. 'Green Fountain' *
H/S 90 × 115 cm (36 × 45 in)
Seedling from *H. kikutii*. Lustrous cascading green mound with leaning scapes of pale lilac flowers from midsummer through to autumn. A very distinctive and excellent green hosta that grows vigorously. The reddish tinge of the petioles is enhanced by planting with the fern *Dryopteris erythrosora*, which unfurls with coppery fronds. Excellent habit for a container and popular with flower arrangers.

H. 'Green Piecrust' *
H/S 70 × 90 cm (28 × 36 in)
Large wavy-edged dark green leaves suggesting a piecrust. Pale lavender flowers in early summer. Would look effective in dappled shade underplanted with epimediums.

H. 'Green Sheen' *
H/S 70 × 100 cm (28 × 40 in)
Good textured, large, pale green leaves with a sheen. Tall stems of pale lavender flowers in late summer. Although green a distinctive, refined plant that makes a very large mound and would be effective pale contrast against *Polystichum braunii* in a green border with *Helleborus corsicus* and *Euphorbia amygdalioides robbiae*.

H. 'Ground Master'
H/S 25 × 55 cm (10 × 22 in)
Undulating lance-shaped, matt green leaf with creamy edge. Tall attractive purple flowers in late summer. Vigorous ground cover and for edging in shade or dappled light. *H.* 'Resonance' is very similar, especially when juvenile. Effective planted under *H. ventricosa* 'Variegata' in a hosta border.

H. 'Ground Sulphur'
H/S 13 × 20 cm (5 × 8 in)
Small lanceolate gold leaves with racemes of pale lavender blooms on 20 cm (8 in) scapes in midsummer. Good grower that appears to stand some sun. One for the alpine bed or the edge of a small bed.

H. 'Hadspen Blue'
H/S 30 × 60 cm (12 × 24 in)
Tardiana group TF 2 × 7. Medium-sized, glaucous blue, thick leaves. Scape purple-dotted at the base with lavender flowers just above the foliage mound in midsummer. Pest-resistant. Slow to mature but when grown in partial shade will eventually be one of the

H. 'Sum and Substance' growing in a pot at Goldbrook Plants,
one of the best hostas for resistance to slug and snail
damage. Excellent large leaves of chartreuse gold.

H. 'Frances Williams' beginning in part to sport to gold.
When this division is removed it becomes *H*. 'Golden
Sunburst', the name given to the sport.

bluest hostas in the garden. Lovely grown with *Dicentra* 'Pearl Drops'.

H. 'Hadspen Heron'
H/S 23×55 cm (9×22 in)
Tardiana group TF 2×10. Small, narrow, glaucous blue-green leaf. Short scape with racemes of pale lavender flowers in midsummer. Emerges early and can be frost damaged. Looks better if divided regularly as is rather untidy when allowed to become a large specimen.

H. 'Halcyon'*
H/S 38×70 cm (15×28 in)
Tardiana group TF 1×7. Very blue, heart-shaped leaves which are even deeper blue in shade. Good lilac-blue flowers on purplish scapes in midsummer. One of the best of the Tardiana group, holding its colour for most of the season. Invaluable in the shade garden and excellent ground cover under shrubs; especially effective with silvery foliage and under shrub roses. One of the few blue hostas that grows well in a pot to maturity. Has given rise to sports, one of which is *H.* 'Goldbrook Glimmer'. This has blue leaves with a cloudy lighter middle, a very unusual colour effect which will be popular with flower arrangers.

H. 'Harmony'
H/S 18×40 cm (7×16 in)
Tardiana group TF 2×3. Similar in leaf shape to *H.* 'Hadspen Heron' but with purple-dotted scapes and purple flowers that are the darkest of the group.

H. 'Holly's Honey'
H/S 45×60 cm (18×24 in)
Shiny dark green, very ruffled leaves similar to *H. ventricosa*. Very tall purple flowers in midsummer. Slow to establish but a very distinct green hosta. Will be popular with flower arrangers when more readily available.

H. 'Honeybells'
H/S 75×120 cm (30×48 in)
Hybrid of *H. plantaginea*. Fresh green, undulating leaves with racemes of fragrant, palest lilac flowers in late summer. Very vigorous and useful for ground cover. Stands more sun than most but not hot and dry.

H. 'Hydon Sunset'
H/S 23×45 cm (9×18 in)
Seedling of *H.* 'Wogon Gold' and *H. gracillima*. Small leaves, gold on emergence which gradually fade to a duller shade. Smooth scapes 30 cm (12 in) tall with deep purple flowers in midsummer. Needs dappled light for best leaf colour as it easily scorches in too much sun. Excellent edger or for a rock garden. *H.* 'Dawn' ('Sunset') is similar although of a different lineage, the gold holding longer, and with fewer veins in the leaf. The base of the scape is slightly ridged, suggesting the possible influence of *H. venusta*. The flowers are slightly paler and more bell-shaped.

H. 'Dawn' has been distributed as *H.* 'Sunset' but this was not a registered name and as it is so easily mixed up with *H.* 'Hydon Sunset', the British Hosta and Hemerocallis Society have decided to register it as *H.* 'Dawn' to differentiate it more clearly. *H.* 'Dawn' is also muddled up in the trade with *H.* 'Wogon Gold' ('Wogon Giboshi'), a poor grower which has more elongated yellow leaves, smooth scapes and flowers with yellow anthers (*H.* 'Dawn' has bluish anthers). *H.* 'Dawn' has recently given rise to a green-rimmed sport called *H.* 'Green with Envy' which should make a very attractive addition to beds planted with small hostas and shade-loving alpines.

H. hypoleuca
H/S 45×90 cm (18×36 in)
Pale green oval leaves with a pronounced white back. Scapes are leaning with trumpet-shaped pale mauve-violet flowers in late summer. Very slow. Needs shade

but stands dryish soils. A recently introduced plant that is very similar is called *H.* 'Maekawa' which forms a symmetrical cascading mound with plenty of lavender flowers just above the foliage in midsummer. Seems more vigorous.

H. 'Inaho'
H/S 25×55 cm (10×22 in)
A *H. lancifolia* form that has masqueraded under many names, including *H. tardiva* and *H. sieboldii* 'Inaho'. Very similar in colour to *H.* 'Chinese Sunrise' but much smaller. Leaves streaked green and gold, with 45 cm (18 in), slightly red-spotted scapes carrying racemes of purple flowers with bluish anthers. Very slow initially but makes a very attractive small mound when mature. Partial sun.

H. 'Invincible'*
H/S 30×60 cm (12×24 in)
Undulating, glossy green leaves that are slug-resistant. Racemes of fragrant light lavender flowers in late summer on 50 cm (20 in) scapes. This is an excellent hosta that deserves to be more widely grown. The leaves are very handsome and distinctive. A lovely subject for the white and green garden and one of the best green leaves for flower arranging. Can make an impressive clump in a container and although it will grow in some sun looks better in dappled light. Very vigorous.

H. 'Iona'
H/S 50×70 cm (20×28 in)
Sport of *H. fortunei*. Greyish cast to the green leaf with a good creamy white margin that holds all season. Plant with *Liriope muscari*. A similar hosta is *H.* 'Sundance', which is the variegated form of *H. fortunei* 'Aoki' but with the creamy margin rather narrow on juvenile plants but increasing in width with age.

H. 'Iron Gate Glamour'
H/S 70×75 cm (28×30 in)
Medium to large leaves are green edged with creamy white. Scapes 90 cm (3 ft) tall with large fragrant lavender flowers in late summer. One of the more recent scented hostas that will become popular. The flowers are pale enough to be used in a white garden that uses pale flowers to enhance the effect. Could be planted with *H.* 'Invincible' and *H.* 'So Sweet' to make a fragrant group that all flower together.

H. 'Janet'
H/S 38×60 cm (15×24 in)
Chartreuse yellow to white leaves with a green edge of a thin texture. Lavender flowers in midsummer. Not the easiest of hostas to grow as it must have dappled shade but popular with flower arrangers and probably best grown in a pot. Similar in appearance to the much more vigorous *H.* 'Gold Standard'.

H. 'June'*
H/S 25×50 cm (10×20 in)
A very recent sport of *H.* 'Halcyon', found in tissue culture by Neoplants. The glaucous gold leaf has a narrow green-blue edge. It is very striking although slow to grow initially. One to use as a specimen in dappled light and will be sought after by flower arrangers once it becomes more widely available. Associate with ferns and gold grasses.

H. kikutii
H/S 40×60 cm (16×24 in)
Slender green leaves with an arching habit. Slightly leaning scapes have reddish petioles with 60 cm (24 in) stems of lavender flowers in early autumn. There are a number of variable forms from the wild and these are being given cultivar names in USA. Elegant foil for variegated hostas and the fluffy flowers of *Smilacina racemosa*.

77

H. 'June', a superb new sport that arose in tissue culture from H. 'Halcyon'.

H. kikutii 'Pruinose' *
H/S 30×50 cm (12×20 in)
The long, very narrow green leaves, reminiscent of *H. longissima*, have a heavy substance and a white back. Scapes to 45 cm (18 in) have a cluster of near-white lavender-tipped flowers in late summer and early autumn. A distinctive, very attractive, slow-growing plant that should be planted where its subtle effect can be appreciated. Should appeal to flower arrangers.

H. 'Krossa Regal' *
H/S 75×100 cm (30×40 in)
Related to *H. nigrescens*. Large, glaucous, blue-grey leaves of a heavy substance that become more green as the season advances. Distinctive, attractive vase-shaped mound. Spires up to 1.5 m (5 ft) of bell-shaped lilac flowers in midsummer. Excellent growth habit, pest-resistant and superb as landscape or container plant. Bloom on the leaf lasts longer in some shade. Effective with *Hakonechloa macra* 'Alboaurea'.

H. lancifolia
H/S 45×75 cm (18×30 in)
Narrow, lanceolate, shiny green leaves form a dense

arching mound. Many racemes of trumpet-shaped deep violet flowers with lilac-blue anthers from late summer through to autumn. The colour of the anthers distinguishes this from *H. sieboldii* which has yellow anthers. Excellent for ground cover and edging. There are some smaller forms in cultivation and *H.* 'Change of Tradition' and *H.* 'New Tradition' are recent variegated sports.

H. 'Leather Sheen'
H/S 35×60 cm (14×24 in)
Dark green, leathery but glossy leaves. Scapes to 75 cm (30 in) with pale lavender flowers in midsummer. A useful foil to brasher plants.

H. **'Brim Cup', a young plant of an excellent new smaller-growing hosta, in association with** *Clematis jouiana* **'Praecox'.**

H. 'Lemon Lime'
H/S 15×45 cm (6×18 in)
Small chartreuse gold, wavy leaves with no purple spots at base of petioles, which distinguishes it from *H.* 'Hydon Sunset', *H.* 'Dawn' ('Sunset') and *H.* 'Wogon Gold', although similar in appearance. Lavender flowers 25 cm (10 in) high from midsummer onwards. A small vigorous hosta for dappled shade.

79

H. 'Little Blue' *
H/S 35×45 cm (14×18 in)
Seedling of *H. ventricosa*. Not small and not blue!
Glossy dark green foliage with tall purple flowers in
midsummer. Much smaller than parent. Attractive
green mound.

H. 'Little White Lines'
H/S 20×45 cm (8×18 in)
Sport of a *H. venusta* seedling. Small mid-green leaves
edged with white. Scapes 50 cm (20 in) tall with purple
flowers in midsummer. Seems vigorous.

H. longipes latifolia hypoglauca
H/S 30×70 cm (12×28 in)
Superb shiny green leaf of a good substance with a
white back. One of the many in this complex and they
are closely related to *H. kikutii*. Characterized by
leaning scapes which are sometimes nearly horizon-
tal. This rare form has very distinctive foliage but is
slow growing with 75 cm (30 in) long slightly leaning
scapes.

H. longissima
H/S 25×50 cm (10×20 in)
Very long, narrow, dull green leaves of a slightly
leathery texture. Strong scapes 55 cm (22 in) tall with
reddish purple funnel-shaped flowers with blue-purple
anthers in late summer. The flowers of *H. sieboldii*,
which is often mistaken for *H. longissima*, have yellow
anthers. I have a form which has much shorter petioles
and flowers that do not have the reddish tinge. This
could be *H. longissima brevifolia* or just another
variant from the wild. Many new forms exist, some
variegated, and are being registered with cultivar
names. Prefers a damp spot, not too shady and should
be placed so that the long narrow leaf is appreciated.

H. 'Love Pat' *
H/S 45×90 cm (18×36 in)

Seedling of *H. tokudama* that is larger than the
species. Very beautiful cupped, glaucous blue leaves
topped with near-white flowers in early summer. A
superb newer hosta which although slow is worth the
wait and is different from *H.* 'Buckshaw Blue',
probably also a *H. tokudama* seedling. Associate with
low-growing shade-loving plants such as *Lamium
maculatum* 'White Nancy' so that the foliage mound
can be appreciated, against a backdrop of *Elaeagnus
angustifolia* 'Caspica' for a blue-silver group. Best not
planted under trees as the leaves will collect all the
detritus.

H. 'Midas Touch' *
H/S 50×65 cm (20×26 in)
Heavy textured gold, dimpled and cupped leaves with
a sheen. Pale lavender flowers 50 cm (20 in) tall in
midsummer. Very slow. Needs some sun to colour and
in cool climates will grow in full sun. Grow with
Molinia caerulea 'Variegata', *Cornus alba* 'Aurea' and
Iris sibirica in moist soil.

H. 'Mildred Seaver' *
H/S 40×60 cm (16×24 in)
Good rounded green leaves of medium size with a
wide creamy yellow margin which becomes white.
Many scapes of pale lavender flowers in midsummer.
Appears vigorous. Best in part shade as highlight to a
green border. Like so many hostas looks lovely with
green ferns such as *Polystichum setiferum* 'Herrenhau-
sen'.

H. minor *
H/S 15×45 cm (6×18 in)
Small, dark green, wavy-edged leaves with 45 cm
(18 in) ridged scapes of attractive mauve funnel-shaped
flowers in midsummer. Larger than the very similar
H. venusta. Needs some shade to grow well and when
happy makes quite rapid mounds for a small hosta.

H. minor 'Alba' is an incorrect name often given to *H. sieboldii* 'Alba'.

H. montana
H/S 100×100 cm (40×40 in)
Large oval, glossy, dark green leaves topped by tall very pale violet funnel-shaped flowers in midsummer. There are many forms of *H. montana* so this description can only be a generalization; some have darker flowers. All are vigorous, large and often superb foliage plants, and have been much used in the raising of a number of hybrids. Many newer forms are being collected in Japan and some have already found their way into specialists' gardens. I do not believe this is the same as *H. elata*, which I feel is probably a hybrid related to *H. fortunei* which it resembles. This is a foliage plant *par excellence* and, like most green hostas, is rarely planted.

H. montana 'Aureo-marginata'*
H/S 70×90 cm (28×36 in)
Huge, pointed green leaves with a wide yellow margin. Much taller near-white flowers in mid-summer. Superb but very slow to establish and as it is the first hosta to emerge is often frost damaged. If carefully sited or grown in a large container protected from early frosts it is one of the most spectacular foliage plants for the gardener and the flower arranger. A white-edged sport of this is called *H.* 'Mountain Snow', and as it also has near-white flowers it could have a future within the white garden, but it is as yet very new and expensive. Grow either hosta with *Dicentra spectabilis* 'Alba' and *Primula denticulata* 'Alba' for a late spring group. The all-gold sport *H.* 'Emma Foster' is very slow and of a weak constitution.

H. 'Moon Glow'*
H/S 40×60 cm (16×24 in)
Seedling of *H.* 'August Moon' with good textured gold leaves edged in white. Mature leaves become cupped and dimpled, the young ones being smooth. Near-white flowers in midsummer. Considered one of the best of this type; vigorous. The white rim is emphasized if contrasted with ferns or could be planted with gold hostas and *Lysimachia nummularia* 'Aurea'. The all-gold sport is called *H.* 'Harvest Glow'.

H. 'Moonlight'*
H/S 50×70 cm (20×28 in)
Sport of *H.* 'Gold Standard'. One of the best of the white-edged gold types. Must have some sun to colour but if too hot will scorch. A striking hosta when well grown; looks good underplanted with small gold hostas with a dark green background.

H. nakaiana
H/S 25×60 cm (10×24 in)
Smallish mound of deep green foliage with purple flowers on ridged scapes in midsummer. Very floriferous. The dimensions given are only a guide to size as many forms exist. Has given rise to many hybrids and seedlings that have been named, such as *H.* 'Bouquet', *H.* 'Candy Hearts', *H.* 'Happy Hearts', *H.* 'Marquis', *H.* 'Pearl Lake' and *H.* 'Valentine Lace', and these make very attractive smaller hostas with excellent flowers.

H. 'Nicola'
H/S 40×75 cm (16×30 in)
Tardiana group. The only named green-leaved hosta in the group. Good dark green, matt leaves with many stems of pinkish flowers in mid to late summer. Very vigorous and is particularly effective with pale pink astilbes underplanting *Acer negundo* 'Flamingo'.

H. nigrescens
H/S 70×90 cm (28×36 in)
Oval, slightly cupped, glaucous leaves are grey-blue

**A large planting of *H. fluctuans* 'Variegated' in Longwood
Gardens, USA.**

83

H. 'Francee', in David Foreman's garden, UK. One of the best
hostas for gardens and pots.

on emergence and greener later. Distinctive, large vase-shaped clump with the leaves having very long stems. Pale lavender flowers in midsummer reach to 1.5 m (5 ft). *H.* 'Krossa Regal' arose from this species.

H. 'Northern Halo'
H/S 70×90 cm (28×36 in)
Tissue culture sport of *H. sieboldiana* 'Elegans'. Bluish corrugated leaves edged white. Near-white flowers in early summer. Most of the *H.* 'Northern Halo' in commerce are of a very cupped form with a narrow white edge and this is inferior to the wide-edged type which was given an award in USA. Expect to find the better form in the future in specialist nurseries. *H.* 'Northern Lights' has a cream-white central blade to the glaucous blue-green leaf. It is very slow and has a tendency to revert.

H. 'On Stage'
H/S 35×60 cm (14×24 in)
Form of *H. montana*. The creamy white leaf is edged with two tones of green with some streaks from the margin into the centre. Blooms in late summer with racemes of lavender flowers. Emerges later than *H. montana* 'Aureo-marginata' and appears reasonably vigorous for a medio-variegated type.

H. 'Osprey'
H/S 23×50 cm (9×20 in)
Tardiana group TF 2×14. Bluish cupped leaves of a thick texture. Good white flowers in midsummer. This is the only white-flowering hosta in the Tardiana group, all the others have some colour in the blooms. Useful for the white garden and very attractive in flower.

H. 'Pastures New'
H/S 30×75 cm (12×30 in)
A *H. nakaiana* cross. Bright grey-green, heart-shaped leaves make a very dense, rapid-growing mound. Many pale lavender flowers are held well above the foliage mound. There seem to be two forms of this in cultivation, one much greener than the other and possibly the better plant. Perhaps this should become *H.* 'Green Pastures' to differentiate it. Flowers slightly later with shorter scapes. Superb planted in a container.

H. 'Pearl Lake'
H/S 38×90 cm (15×36 in)
Dense mound of heart-shaped, green-grey foliage. Abundant lavender flowers on 80 cm (32 in) purplish stems from early summer onwards. A delightful hosta whether planted in the garden or in a container. Vigorous. Very useful as an edger in pink, blue and white colour borders.

H. 'Piedmont Gold'
H/S 50×90 cm (20×36 in)
Large crinkle-edged gold leaves. Mature plants have an attractive habit. Pale lavender or near-white flowers on scapes just above the leaf mound in early to midsummer. Needs partial shade as it will become papery in too much sun. Colours well in dappled light. When well grown one of the best of the larger golds. A recent sport with a white margin to the gold leaves is *H.* 'Evening Magic', which will probably not grow quite so large.

H. 'Pizzazz'
H/S 50×75 cm (20×30 in)
Very heavy, textured, heart-shaped blue-green leaves with a variable margin of creamy yellow. Many racemes of pale lavender flowers in mid to late summer. Best in shade or dappled light. One to look out for as it appears distinct. Will need careful placing, probably with blues and golds. Good with *Carex* 'Frosted Curls'.

H. plantaginea
H/S 60×100 cm (24×40 in)
Light green, oval, glossy leaves with scapes of very fragrant tubular trumpet-shaped white flowers 10–15 cm (4–6 in) long in autumn. Must have a sunny, moist site to flower. Can be grown in a large container in a fairly sunny spot. It has given rise to a number of forms and sports, the latest of which are as yet not readily available: H. 'Aphrodite' has double flowers, H. 'Chelsea Ore' a mainly gold leaf with a green rim and in cooler climates needs to be grown in a pot. H. 'White Shoulders' has a narrow white edge to the green leaf, and H. 'Venus' has more petals in the flowers than H. 'Aphrodite'.

H. pycnophylla
H/S 30×70 cm (12×28 in)
Species that is rare in gardens but very useful for hybridizing. Pale grey-green, wavy leaves with a pronounced white back. Leaning, slightly purple-dotted flowering stem with pale mauve trumpet-shaped blooms. Slow to establish and best with some shade. Seems to grow well in a pot. Handsome.

H. 'Regal Splendor'*
H/S 75×100 cm (30×40 in)
Tissue culture sport of H. 'Krossa Regal'. Slow in early years but eventually an excellent large, vase-shaped specimen with leaves that are greyish blue with a good cream margin. Tall light lavender flowers. A very distinctive newer hosta. Plant with lower-growing blue hostas and Dicentra 'Pearl Drops'.

H. 'Reversed'*
H/S 35×65 cm (14×26 in)
Blue-green foliage with large creamy centre. Attractive flowers. Needs some shade and time to build up vigour. Makes a good container plant and repays feeding and care. Excellent for the flower arranger. A very

lovely hosta when well grown and one that is best watered underneath. Group with ferns.

H. rohdeifolia
H/S 30×45 cm (12×18 in)
(H. rohdeifolia 'Aureo-marginata', formerly called H. helonioides 'Albo-picta'.) Lance-shaped green leaf, edged yellow fading to white. Purplish flowers in midsummer well above the foliage mound. H. helonioides 'Albo-picta' is similar but the edge is white on unfurling and not yellow.

H. 'Royal Standard'
H/S 60×120 cm (24×48 in)
A hybrid from H. plantaginea. Fairly large bright green leaves offset the scented, trumpet-shaped white flowers which appear on 90 cm (3 ft) scapes in late summer. As long as the soil is moist it will be happy in all but the hottest sun. Excellent for the white garden and for ground cover as it grows rapidly. Some double flowering forms have been discovered; expect these to be named shortly.

H. 'Royalty'
H/S 25×35 cm (10×14 in)
The small gold leaves are pointed with dark purple flowers in late summer. Striking and quite vigorous.

H. rupifraga
H/S 20×60 cm (8×24 in)
Distinctive, medium-sized, heart-shaped leaves are a glossy pale green, very thick and leathery with undulations. Attractive pale purple, bell-shaped flowers from early autumn onwards. Forms vary slightly from the wild. Excellent hosta; true forms are rarely available.

H. 'Saishu Jima'
H/S 8×38 cm (3×15 in)
Form of H. sieboldii. Small, green, very narrow leaves

H. 'Iona' growing in the garden of Jackie Rowan in Ampfield,
Hampshire, UK. Looks good all season.

87

H. 'Royal Standard', a reliable white-flowering scented
hosta.

with ruffles; 25 cm (10 in) pale purple flowers in late summer. Suitable for alpine beds and as a small edger. A very similar but slightly larger hosta is *H.* 'Haku-jima'.

H. 'Sea Dream'
H/S 60 × 70 cm (20 × 28 in)
Leaves are bright gold with a white margin. Tall lavender flowers in midsummer. Must have some shade. Like all white-edged golds, looks best with golds, whites and greens.

H. 'Sea Drift' *
H/S 60 × 90 cm (24 × 36 in)
Good-textured pie-crusted green leaves that appeal to flower arrangers. Tall scapes, to 90 cm (3 ft), with lavender-pink flowers in midsummer. Slow to establish and not suitable for a pot.

H. 'Sea Gold Star' *
H/S 50 × 75 cm (20 × 30 in)
Dimpled, very heavy textured bright gold leaves with 90 cm (3 ft) near-white flowers in midsummer. Very slow to become established and needs four or five years before it starts to reveal its potential. Some sun to colour but not the midday sun. Superb foliage when mature.

H. 'Sea Lotus Leaf' *
H/S 45 × 60 cm (18 × 24 in)
Glossy dark blue-green rounded leaves that are so cupped that the water collects in each leaf. Very pale lavender to near-white bell-shaped flowers in midsummer just above the leaf mound. Slow but distinctive foliage plant. Needs to be sited away from tree drip.

H. 'Sea Monster'
H/S 65 × 100 cm (26 × 40 in)
Corrugated green leaves of a good substance that make a large mound. Near-white blooms in early summer.

H. 'Sea Octopus'
H/S 23 × 55 cm (9 × 22 in)
Narrow green leaves with undulating margins. Scapes 80 cm (32 in) high have purple flowers in early autumn. Vigorous smaller hosta suitable for edging and as a foil to variegated hostas with similar leaf shape such as *H. sieboldii*.

H. 'Shade Fanfare' *
H/S 45 × 60 cm (18 × 24 in)
In the early season the green leaf has a wide creamy margin but as the season advances more yellow tones develop if the plant is in some sun but not if grown in shade. Stems 60 cm (24 in) tall of lavender flowers in midsummer. Vigorous, easy cultivar already very popular with gardeners and flower arrangers. Grow with *Miscanthus sinensis* 'Zebrinus' for an intriguing contrast of texture, form and variegation in a place shaded from the hottest sun of the day. Looks good with *Digitalis ambigua, Helleborus corsicus* and erythroniums in a shady green and cream scheme.

H. 'Shining Tot'
H/S 5 × 20 cm (2 × 8 in)
Tiny, shiny, deep green leaves of a good substance. One of the smallest hostas. Light blue trumpet-shaped flowers on 13 cm (5 in) arching scapes in summer. Best in partial shade although will tolerate sun in all but the hottest places. A delightful little plant that is a good increaser but needs to be seen close up on a raised bed.

H. sieboldiana 'Elegans' *
H/S 90 × 125 cm (36 × 50 in)
The best known of the many *H. sieboldiana* forms. Very large, heart-shaped, cupped and puckered bluish leaves that are pest-resistant. Trumpet-shaped

lavender-white flowers just above the foliage mound in early summer. Best in partial shade as the bloom on the leaf is retained for longer but remarkably effective in a moist spot even in some sun. One of the most popular hostas and extremely useful in many situations in the garden. A slightly smaller cultivar is *H.* 'Helen Doriot' which has similar coloured flowers. One with whiter flowers is called *H.* 'Blue Seer' which, although slow, is a very impressive plant in a shady spot and suitable for the white garden. There are many named selections; all are good garden plants.

H. sieboldii

H/S 30 × 60 cm (12 × 24 in)
Often called *H. albomarginata* which is incorrect. Lance-shaped, matt green leaves irregularly edged white. Trumpet-shaped violet flowers with yellow anthers in late summer. Quickly makes dense clumps and is very useful for edging in partial shade. There are many forms and named seedlings which have been selected for improved foliage or flowers but generally they are not as vigorous as the type. The best known are *H.* 'Louisa' and *H.* 'Emerald Isle', both with white flowers and green leaves edged white.

H. sieboldii 'Alba'

H/S 13 × 30 cm (5 × 12 in)
Often erroneously called *H. minor* 'Alba'. Small green lanceolate leaves with tallish white flowers from mid-summer to early autumn. Not strong growing. *H.* 'Bianca', *H.* 'Snowflakes' and *H.* 'Weihenstephan' are named selections with larger white flowers and a more vigorous habit.

H. sieboldii 'Kabitan'

H/S 25 × 45 cm (10 × 18 in)
Small, lance-shaped, thin textured, ruffled yellow leaves with a green margin. Tallish trumpet-shaped deep purple flowers in midsummer. When well grown

very distinctive but must have some shade as it will scorch in sun. Seems a much better plant in USA than in Britain. Best grown in pot to establish.

H. sieboldii 'Shiro-kabitan'

H/S 20 × 38 cm (8 × 15 in)
Also erroneously known as *H.* 'Haku Chu Han'. Small lanceolate white leaves have a wide green margin. Purplish flowers well above the leaf mound in mid-summer. Very slow to grow and best in a pot in partial shade until established. When well grown is a delightful little hosta. *H.* 'Squiggles' appears similar but with a larger white centre to the green leaf and lovely white flowers on pale cream scapes 30 cm (12 in) high. Probably best grown in a pot in partial shade.

H. 'Silver Lance'

H/S 30 × 50 cm (12 × 20 in)
Very long, narrow, dark green leaves with a narrow white margin. makes a slightly cascading mound. Racemes of deep lavender flowers 60 cm (24 in) tall from late summer through to autumn. Elegant smaller hosta that needs careful placing to be appreciated.

H. 'Snow Cap'*

H/S 40 × 60 cm (16 × 24 in)
Blue leaves have a wide creamy white edge and are of good substance. Whitish flowers. Will need to grow in shade for best colour. Gives a lovely accent with blue-foliaged dicentras and smaller blue hostas and will appeal to flower arrangers.

H. 'Snowden'*

H/S 90 × 100 cm (36 × 40 in)
Raised by Eric Smith from *H. sieboldiana* and *H. fortunei* 'Aurea'. Large glaucous grey-blue leaves gradually change to grey-green. When happy makes a large mound. Many scapes with bell-shaped white flowers in midsummer. Slow to start but given good cultural conditions, dappled shade and plenty of

H. 'Zounds', an excellent gold in association with *Molinia caerulea*, *Cornus alba* 'Aurea' and *H*. 'Frances Williams' in the distance.

H. 'Sea Drift', a piecrust hosta in Longwood Gardens, USA.

moisture this is a spectacular plant for the garden and flower arranger. I have found it makes a superb container plant and is ideal for the white garden underplanted with white hardy geraniums or *Pulmonaria* 'Sissinghurst White'.

H. 'So Sweet'*
H/S 35×55 cm (14×22 in)
Glossy green leaves with variable creamy white margin which begins creamy yellow. Fragrant white flowers on 60 cm (24 in) scapes, the buds faintly tipped with lavender in late summer. This is a lovely variety, great in the white garden and for flower arranging. One of the new hostas that is distinctive and very pretty. Plant with *Aruncus aethusifolius*, small ferns and white violets in shade or dappled light.

H. 'Spritzer'*
H/S 45×35 cm (18×14 in)
Lanceolate leaves are two tones of green with a yellow to cream centre. It grows upright and arches over with the same type of habit as *H.* 'Green Fountain', which is one of its parents. White flowers tinged bluish purple on 75 cm (30 in) scapes from midsummer onwards. Very elegant in dappled light against *Cornus alba* 'Aurea' and *Hakonechloa macra* 'Alboaurea' underplanted with *Lysimachia nummularia* 'Aurea'. Relatively pest-resistant and will stand more sun than most; best in dappled light.

H. 'Stiletto'
H/S 15×20 cm (6×8 in)
Undulating, very narrow lance-shaped leaves are green with a narrow white rim. Scapes 30 cm (12 in) tall with lavender flowers in late summer. Interesting but as yet little-known hosta.

H. 'Sugar and Cream'*
H/S 60×100 cm (24×40 in)
A tissue culture sport of *H.* 'Honeybells'. A far superior plant with a cream edge to the green leaf. Pale lilac-white fragrant flowers in summer. This has vigour, a good habit and is very easy to mix with other foliage plants. It makes an elegant container plant but needs a large pot.

H. 'Sum and Substance'
H/S 75×120 cm (30×48 in)
Huge chartreuse gold, thick, glossy leaves of a heavy substance. Very impressive and nearly slug-proof. Tall lavender flowers in late summer. Looks good underplanted with small gold hostas or used as an architectural specimen among lower-growing foliage plants. Needs some sun to colour and as long as it is not too dry will stand nearly full sun. One of the largest-leaved hostas and one of the most spectacular.

H. 'Summer Fragrance'
H/S 60×90 cm (24×36 in)
Seedling of *H. plantaginea* (crossed with an unknown hosta). Cream-white margin to a slightly wavy green leaf. Tall scapes with large, beautiful, scented bluish flowers in late summer. Best in shade or dappled light. Good grower. Place in the garden where the fragrance will be appreciated.

H. 'Sun Power'
H/S 60×90 cm (24×36 in)
Large, slightly twisted, golden ruffled leaves with an upright habit. Pale lavender flowers in midsummer, 90 cm (3 ft) high. Needs dappled light to colour and takes time to make an impressive specimen.

H. 'Tall Boy'
H/S 50×90 cm (20×36 in)
Hybrid of *H. rectifolia*. Leaves green and relatively close to the ground. Not particularly good foliage but has a superb flowering display with very tall scapes of deep purplish blue flowers for many weeks in summer. Spectacular when used *en masse* for ground cover.

H. tardiflora *
H/S 25 × 60 cm (10 × 24 in)
Lance-shaped, dark green, lustrous leaves with a heavy substance. Lavender-purple, trumpet-shaped flowers on red stems just above the foliage in early autumn. Excellent for the front of the border and very underrated.

H. 'Tiny Tears'
H/S 8 × 15 cm (3 × 6 in)
Seedling of H. venusta. Tiny green leaves form a very small mound for the rock grden in partial shade. Purple flowers in midsummer. H. 'Thumb Nail' is similar but even smaller with light blue trumpet flowers on a 25 cm (10 in) scape.

H. tokudama *
H/S 35 × 90 cm (14 × 36 in)
Heavily textured, cupped and puckered blue leaves. Trumpet-shaped greyish white flowers in midsummer just above the foliage mound. Very slow but distinctive hosta that prefers shade (not under trees) and useful in the white garden.

H. tokudama 'Aureo-nebulosa' *
H/S 30 × 55 cm (12 × 22 in)
Leaves have an irregular cloudy yellow centre with a bluish margin. Leaf colour is variable and some forms are far better than others. Scapes 60 cm (2 ft) tall have clusters of whitish blooms from early to midsummer. Eye-catching variety very popular with flower arrangers although very slow to increase. H. 'Goldbrook Gift' is a sport with a bluish leaf and a yellow margin narrower than H. tokudama 'Flavo-circinalis'. H. 'Winning Edge' is a selfed H. tokudama 'Aureo-nebulosa' with a wide cream edge to green-blue centre.

H. tokudama 'Flavo-circinalis' *
H/S 45 × 75 cm (18 × 30 in)
Heart-shaped blue leaves with a wide creamy yellow margin, more pointed than H. tokudama. Looks like a small H. 'Frances Williams' but has a pale lavender flower with darker stripes slightly later and the leaves are not as cupped when mature. Superb but slow.

H. undulata 'Albo-marginata' *
H/S 55 × 90 cm (22 × 36 in)
Commonly known as H. 'Thomas Hogg'. Wavy, white-edged green leaves with rather flat petioles. Often muddled with H. crispula which has more undulate leaves and petioles that are narrow and grooved. Pale purple flowers on 90 cm (3 ft) scapes in early summer. Rapid developer and grows nearly anywhere. Excellent under trees and as a container plant. Plant with Solomon's seal, Geranium phaeum album and pulmonaria.

H. undulata 'Erromena'
H/S 50 × 75 cm (20 × 30 in)
Mid-green, wavy, tapering leaves with 90 cm (3 ft) attractive pale mauve flowers in early summer. Multiplies well and makes good ground cover.

H. undulata 'Univittata' *
H/S 38 × 70 cm (15 × 28 in)
Wavy, oval green leaf with a central cream blade. Violet flowers in early summer. Reasonably vigorous and very distinctive in summer. Reliable under trees. As the foliage is so distinct, needs careful placing or can look fussy. Good with green hostas and with the soft shield fern, Polystichum setiferum. H. undulata undulata has a very wide cream centre to the leaf and is not very vigorous. There are many named forms but those with very narrow medio-variegation often revert to green as they are unstable.

H. 'Vanilla Cream'
H/S 13 × 25 cm (5 × 10 in)
Small lemon-green leaves of heavy substance, with slightly reddish scapes 30 cm (12 in) tall carrying

93

lavender flowers in midsummer. Slow growing and suitable for alpine beds in dappled light.

H. ventricosa*
H/S 50×90 cm (20×36 in)
Heart-shaped, slightly wavy, dark green glossy leaves. Good 90 cm (3ft), deep purple bell-shaped flowers in late summer. Excellent green mound that is very effective under variegated shrubs such as *Elaeagnus ebbingei* 'Limelight'. *H. ventricosa* 'Aureo-maculata' has a central gold splash to the green leaf which fades later. Not very vigorous and smaller growing.

H. ventricosa 'Variegata'*
H/S 50×90 cm (20×36 in)
(Registered in USA as *H. ventricosa* 'Aureo-margin-ata'.) The dark green leaves have a striking creamy yellow edge that becomes whiter as the season advances. Excellent racemes of deep purple flowers in late summer. Although slow initially, when mature it is one of the most spectacular of the variegated hostas.

H. venusta
H/S 8×25 cm (3×10 in)
Small heart-shaped, darkish green leaves. Many funnel-shaped lavender-violet flowers on 25 cm (10 in) ridged scapes in midsummer. Delightful, vigorous little hosta that is very easy to grow in partial shade. Has given rise to many named seedlings such as *H.* 'Tiny Tears', *H.* 'Thumb Nail' with lilac flowers, and *H.* 'Po Po' which has a more rounded leaf. Very ruffled *H. venusta* seedlings and crosses are being selected for naming.

H. venusta 'Variegated'
H/S 8×15 cm (3×6 in)
Probably a hybrid as the scapes are not ridged. The tiny leaves have two tones of green with creamy centres. Lavender flowers on very pale scapes often with a green streak appear in midsummer well above the leaf mound. Best grown in a pot until established although for such a small plant is relatively vigorous. Lovely with the filigree foliage of tiny ferns and *Aruncus aethusifolius*.

H. 'Vera Verde'
H/S 15×38 cm (6×15 in)
Formerly called *H. gracillima* 'Variegated'. Small lance-shaped matt green leaves, edged white. Lavender flowers in midsummer. Stoloniferous. Useful edger for borders and rock gardens in all but full sun.

H. 'Wide Brim'*
H/S 45×90 cm (18×36 in)
Blue-green leaves have a very wide creamy gold band that fades to cream as the season advances. The edge gets wider with age until it is more than half the leaf. Attractive lavender flowers in midsummer. Best in shade or dappled light. Excellent cultivar. Good for flower arrangers.

H. 'Yellow River'
H/S 45×60 cm (18×24 in)
Pointed, heart-shaped, slightly wavy, dark green leaf with a good yellow margin. Lavender flowers in midsummer. Looks good with *Alchemilla mollis* and *Asarum europaeum*.

H. 'Zounds'*
H/S 55×70 cm (22×28 in)
Form of *H. sieboldiana*. Large, rugose gold leaves are puckered and develop a metallic sheen with age; a fine specimen plant for light shade. Pale lavender flowers 75 cm (30 in) high in early summer. Slow. *H.* 'Dick Ward' is a recent sport with a green rim to the gold leaf.

Index

Page numbers in *italics* indicate an illustration; page numbers in **bold** indicate a main hosta entry in the A–Z section.

95

ACKNOWLEDGEMENTS

The publishers are grateful to the following for granting permission to reproduce the colour photographs: Simeon Bond (pp. 7, 10, 30, 46, 51, 59, 62, 66, 67 & 79); John Newbold (pp. 2, 27 & 86); Ali Pollock (p. 14); John Fielding (pp. 19, 22, 34, 39, 54, 71, 75, 83 & 87); Roger Phillips (pp. 42, 74 & 90); Dr. Ulrich Fischer (pp. 70, 82 & 91); and Neoplants Ltd. (p. 78).

Line drawings by Carole Robson   Planting plans by Taurus Graphics